THE OFFICIAL® PRICE GUIDE TO A

THE OFFICIAL® PRICE GUIDE TO

Automobilia

David K. Bausch

First Edition

■

House of Collectibles

NEW YORK

Copyright © 1996 by David K. Bausch

All rights reserved under the International and Pan-American Copyright Conventions.

H This is a registered trademark of Random House, Inc.

Published by: House of Collectibles
201 East 50th Street
New York, NY 10022

Distributed by Ballantine Books, a division of Random House, Inc., New York, and simultaneously in Canada by Random House of Canada Limited, Toronto.

http://www.randomhouse.com

Manufactured in the United States of America

ISSN: 1090-9869

ISBN: 0-676-60030-1

Cover design by Dreu Pennington-McNeil
Cover photo by George Kerrigan
Text design by Mary A. Wirth

First Edition: October 1996

10 9 8 7 6 5 4 3 2 1

I dedicate this book to Dr. Elmer H. and Mrs. Winifred Bausch, my mother and dad. My parents did everything possible to encourage my love of the automobile. They supported me when I bought my first car at age sixteen and tore it apart—first to understand the mechanics of its operation and second to restore it to its original beauty. They helped me contact and meet early automobile inventors and other individuals who worked in the automobile industry.

My parents said nary a word about those whiffs of gasoline and exhaust fumes that seeped into the kitchen, along with the occasional puffs of gray smoke emanating from our attached garage. I am certain that I awoke them many times as a result of my early-morning visits to the garage to spend just a few quick minutes working on the car.

I acknowledge the numerous times my mother said, "I hope you know what you are doing." I am delighted that she lived long enough to understand that the answer was yes.

Special thanks to James and Elmer, Junior, my older brothers, who, as they went off to college and married, relinquished their space in our family home, space that I eagerly usurped for storage of my ever-growing collection of automobile magazines, books, and collectibles.

Last, but not least, I thank those collectors, writers, and automobile pioneers, from inventors to mechanics, who have made my years of automobile collecting fun and so richly rewarding.

CONTENTS

ACKNOWLEDGMENTS

COMTE GEOFFROY DE BEAUFFORT, Brussels, Belgium—a super friend and fellow collector who has spent endless hours with me at the Paris flea markets and antique shops throughout France and Belgium searching for those ever-elusive automobile objects.

JAMES BARRON—who first introduced me to the wonderful world of automobile art.

PETER RICHLY—a friend and walking encyclopedia of automobile history.

KEITH FLETCHER—the world's authority on steam-propelled vehicles.

D. B. TUBBS—writer, auto collector, and author of *Art and the Automobile*.

Those collector-dealers such as CHARLES SCHALEBAUM, TOM SAGE, BILL WEART, and others, who managed to keep me on the edge of bankruptcy. It's been fun!

JOHN ZOLOMIJ—a friend and fellow auto enthusiast. John Zolomij is more pragmatic than I. If the price is right, he buys and sells it. Me, I like to make a lifetime commitment to my things and the hobby. John Zolomij did a wonderful service to the collecting fraternity when he researched Raymond E. Holland's collection of automobile objects and provided the text for *The Motor Car in Art*.

HARRY L. RINKER—educator, antique authority, appraiser, and all-around good guy, who encouraged me to undertake this project. He also edited the manuscript. The good news is that we are still friends.

HARRY RINKER, JR.—collector and photographer. He carefully photographed each and every item in this book.

LORI LIZZA—the individual who successfully transcribed my hen scratches and corrected my Pennsylvania German phrasing.

RANDY LADENHEIM-GIL, the staff of House of Collectibles, and the production group at Ballantine Books for taking the raw material that I submitted and making it into a finished product.

My deepest thanks to all of the above, those I may have inadvertently missed, and finally, you, the reader. Hopefully you will receive as much pleasure from looking through this book as I have received from acquiring, selecting, and working with the objects found in it.

THE OFFICIAL® PRICE GUIDE TO AUTOMOBILIA

Confessions of an Automobilia Collector

I was born to collect. I cannot tell you when I began to collect because I cannot remember ever not collecting. Relative to my interest in automobiles and automobilia, two events in my youth served as catalysts for my lifetime interest in these two subjects.

One of the earliest automobiles made in America was produced in Allentown, Pennsylvania, my hometown. The Nadig, with its 2-cylinder, gasoline-fired, water-cooled engine, first appeared on the streets of Allentown in 1891. My father regaled me with stories about the early days of the Nadig.

The second event that sealed my fate as an automobile collector was a wonderful colored print picturing a 1910 red Model "T" Ford coming out of a barn that appeared in *Ford Times*. That did it! I had to own one. My search began. I soon found a 1913 Model "T" covered with all kinds of useless reusable items—egg cartons, faded awnings, and a few flags—parked in a garage within six blocks of my home. All in all, the car was in remarkably good condition.

The thrill of finding a good period car sequestered in a barn or garage is now almost extinct. Restoring these sleeping beauties is no longer commonplace either. I restored the 1913 Ford Model "T." It is still part of my antique automobile collection.

When unrestored antique automobiles became difficult to find and restoration costs rose, I shifted my principal collecting focus to automobile collectibles. I had been collecting these items during the period when I was restoring antique automobiles. As a result, I had an established base to build upon.

I am often asked to identify the first piece of automobilia I purchased for my collection. My postcard collecting interests predated my automobile and automobilia interests. My postcard collection was broad. It consisted of comic, greeting, holiday, scenic, and many other types of cards. Surprise, surprise: Many of these cards featured automobile images. At the time, I never thought of them as automobilia.

I remember the first automobilia I bought. I was serving in the Air Force and stationed in Georgia. I went to an antique show in Atlanta and purchased four items—a small bisque bottle in the shape of an automobile and three Royal Doulton ceramic plates picturing automobiles. The bottle cost $15, and the plates were $25 each. I still have them.

Over forty-five years later, these initial four automobile collectibles have been joined by an army of others. I am hooked, and I admit it. As my collection has grown, it has become harder and harder for me to find new items. Many of the examples I see, I already own. However, I am pleased to say that my goal of adding at least one new item a week continues to be feasible.

The most prized possessions I found in my travels are not in my collection. They are the people I have met through the years. I was fortunate enough to meet and talk with many early automobile pioneers. I have great memories of sitting for hours listening to tinkers, engineers, blacksmiths, carriage makers, and dreamers recount the early days of motoring.

I remember Mr. Nadig telling me of the day when he drove his automobile up Hamilton Street in Allentown and frightened Col. Young's high-stepping horse. He was arrested for disturbing the peace. He shared his tale about the day when his brakes failed, the gas tank caught on fire, and half of the car was burned.

Mr. Nadig said that the people came running out of the doors to see what was making all the noise. They stood in awe as his "thrashing machine," as they called it, passed by.

Nadig's first country trips surprised many farmers. Some stopped their plowing and stared in awe. Others ran into the house to call everyone to come out and see this new curiosity. At one farmhouse, a woman stood at the water pump. When she saw Nadig coming down the hill, she yelled, "There is a wagon running away without a horse!" He had many stories about the early days of motoring.

Mr. Sourwine, a Slatington, Pennsylvania, mechanic, built a steam wagon in his barn. When it was finished, it was so large he had to remove the barn doors to get it out.

Nadig, Sourwine, and the others are gone now. I deeply regret that I did not use a tape recorder to capture their stories for posterity. Fortunately, they are part of my memory, and I am well aware of the importance of its verbal transmission. I pass along these stories to younger collectors every chance I get.

I treasure my interactions with the early pioneers of automobile and automobilia collecting. Four individuals who come immediately to mind are Comte Geoffroy de Beauffort of Belgium and Jim Barron, Peter Richly, and D. B. Tubbs of England.

The way I met some of these foreign collectors is an interesting story. *Stardust,* a small English publication about the size of *Ford Times,* carried an advertisement from an English collector seeking old automobile posters. If he could find automobile posters, perhaps I could find other automobile collectibles. I placed an advertisement.

A few months later, I heard from Jim Barron. No one had replied to his advertisement so he decided to write to me. Material flowed between our two collections for quite some time.

While in England visiting Jim Barron, I went to see Keith Fletcher, owner of a London bookstore and collector of automobile-related books. In walked a French-speaking group. Comte Geoffroy de Beauffort, a major collector of automobile books and collectibles, was a member of that group. De Beauffort had authored several books on the subject. He carried with him a photograph album of his extensive collection of pocket watches whose cases featured automobile images. I had a watch case in my collection not pictured in his book and I offered it to him. Up to this point, the conversation was in French. When I made my offer and de Beauffort accepted, the conversation switched to English. De Beauffort extended an invitation to visit his castle in Belgium. I accepted. We have been good friends ever since and never out of touch.

Where does the fun of collecting reside—in owning the object or in the search for it? Al Marwick, a writer about toys, always says, "The fun is in the search." I agree up to a point. For me, joy comes knowing that an object exists and then seeing it. I do not always have to own it. Seeing it is the catharsis.

Collectors tell tales of the hunt just as hunters do. Here are two of my favorites. While in Europe during one of my periodic buying trips, Geoffroy de Beauffort suggested we visit the Paris Swiss Market, a small shopping center of antique shops. I was looking for a nodding-head chauffeur for my collection, and de Beauffort said he had seen one in a shop. We arrived early Monday morning, the first customers in the door. There was a bisque nodder, but it was priced higher than I was willing to pay. I did not buy it, and we left the shop. De Beauffort suggested that I go back and make a counteroffer. It is a suggestion that I continue to thank him for to this day.

We went back. As we walked through the door, there was one of the most magnificent automobile collectibles I have ever seen—a ceramic vase made for Moto Bloc for display at the 1907 Paris automobile show. When we had been in the shop earlier, the salesperson had stood in front of the vase. De Beauffort said, "Either you purchase it or I will." I bought it. It sat on my lap during the 747 flight back to the United States. Today, it sits in my home office.

Although this book is about automobilia, I am compelled to share the story of how I acquired my most historic automobile. While driving around looking for automobilia, I passed a home and a group of greenhouses in front of which stood a cement owl. As a young boy, my father often drove by what was left of the Nadig machine shop. It had a cement owl in front of it. Could it be the same owl?

I stopped and went up to the front door of the house and knocked. A gentleman answered. I introduced myself. The person said his last name was Nadig. I shared my story about the Nadig car and the cement owl with him.

"I suppose you want to see the car," he said. You could have knocked me over with a feather. I had always believed the car was lost when a fire destroyed the Nadig machine shop in the 1930s. I saw the car and left.

Years later I helped organize the Das Awkscht Fescht (August Fest) antique car show. Knowing that the first Nadig existed and that I did not own it weighed heavily on my mind. Eventually, I went and talked to the relative who owned the car. The building in which it was housed had collapsed in the interim. My heart sank. Undaunted and trusting my skills of verbal persuasion, I started talking and did not stop until I acquired what was left of the Nadig.

During the course of restoring the Nadig, I needed to find new wheels. The old wheels had rotted. Hoops Brothers Darlington, a manufacturer of wooden wheels located in West Chester, Pennsylvania, was still in business. I took a hub to show the foreman. He looked at it closely, went into a large room, climbed a ladder that moved around the room on a track, and pulled down a ledger. He looked up the number that was on the hub of my Nadig wheel and matched it with one in his book. Hoops Brothers Darlington had made the original wheels in 1889 for the M. S. Young Hardware Company in Allentown, the source from which Nadig had purchased them.

What serendipity! Hoops Brothers Darlington is no more. The factory is now an apartment house. Yet another early chapter in automobile history lost.

I wrote this book in spurts. I authored the chapter on collecting tips as I and the mosquitoes sat by the roadside in Cherryville waiting for road service for one of my old cars. I frequently take my cars out for a ride in the country. Sometimes we arrived home. This time we did not.

My car experienced electrical problems, and I could not correct them. I called for assistance from a service garage with explicit instructions that if they could not get the old steed revived, it should be hauled on a flatbed truck and not towed.

As the tow truck arrived, the young driver remarked, "I never saw such an old car. Does it run on gas?" I knew I was in trouble. I asked him to return and bring the rollback. You do not tow a car with a laminated ash frame with a modern wrecker.

I am back home and all is well. The venerable steed is sleeping until our next uncharted adventure. Finishing this introduction ends my writing responsibilities.

Before putting my last words on paper, I decided to take a minute and glance around at my automobilia. The wonderful thing about them is that they remind me of the pluses and minuses associated with my collection without my ever having to worry about the mosquitoes.

Now that I am done, I think I will go out to my garden and admire the Nadig cement owl.

1.

A BRIEF HISTORY OF THE AUTOMOBILE AND AUTOMOBILIA COLLECTING

It is impossible to collect automobile collectibles, also known as automobilia and mobilia, without becoming intimately involved with the history of the automobile. Historical information is the key to dating automobilia. Fortunately, most collectors are versed in automobile history. Unfortunately, they know little about the history of automobile collecting. This is why this chapter includes two brief histories—the history of the automobile and the history of automobilia.

History of the Automobile

A hundred years have passed since the first internal combustion engine automobile was manufactured in the United States. Those who envisioned the automobile as the way of the future overcame those who opposed it as a noisy, smelly contraption that would lead to the downfall of civilization.

In 1772 Oliver Evans, an American inventor, proposed the building of a steam-driven carriage. Early in 1805 he demonstrated a steam-driven dredge, the Orukter Amphivolos, based upon his steam carriage idea. The dredge worked; the steam carriage was washed away in the tides of history.

Several English inventors, like F. Hill, Francis Macerone, and John Squire, were successful in their efforts to manufacture steam-driven carriages. Concerned about the speed of these new monsters, Britain passed its 1865 Red Flag laws that limited speed to not more than four miles per hour in the country and two miles per hour in the city and required a walking attendant to carry a red warning flag preceding the vehicle. The law remained in effect until 1896, preventing Britain from becoming a major force in the development of the automobile.

In 1860 Etienne Lenoir, a Belgian living in Paris, developed the first successful internal combustion engine. His double-acting, two-cycle engine burned a mixture of air and coal gas.

In 1872 George B. Brayton, a Boston engineer, patented a two-cycle combustion engine that featured a single cylinder and burned a distillate of kerosene called gasoline. As a result of Brayton's patent, the federal government proposed in 1875 the formation of a Horseless Carriage Commission on the grounds that never before had America "been confronted with a power so full of potential danger and at the same time so full of promise for the future of men and for the peace of the world." Nothing happened.

Brayton demonstrated his engine at the 1876 Centennial Fair in Philadelphia, where it was seen by attorney George B. Selden. Selden eventually bought Brayton's patent rights. In 1879 Selden applied for a patent for a two-cycle, liquid hydro-carbon, internal combustion engine. Because of this patent, most early American automobile manufacturers paid royalties to Selden. It was not until Henry Ford challenged the patent in court that Selden's grip on the industry was broken. Ford won, claiming his cars featured a four-cycle engine, as did most of the cars at that time, and, therefore, did not infringe on two-cycle engine patent.

The history of the four-cycle engine requires a return to Europe. Nicholas Otto, a German, set out to improve Lenoir's engine. His "Ottocycle" or "Silent Otto" was a four-cycle (intake, compression, power, and exhaust) stationary engine, patented in 1876. Carl Benz married the Otto four-cycle engine to a three-wheeled vehicle and patented the concept in 1886. The internal combustion engine automobile was born.

Automobile history divides into two parts at this point: (1) engineering and other technological advances relating to the automobile and (2) the development of roads upon which it could run.

ENGINEERING HIGHLIGHTS

1889 John Dunlop patents first pneumatic tire in Ireland

1901 Curved-dash Oldsmobile, first U.S. car made in quantity

1908 Cadillac makes the first car to use interchangeable parts

1911 Charles Kettering installs first self-starter in Cadillac, widening the door for female drivers

1913 First moving production line installed at Ford's Highland Park plant with a capacity of 1,000 cars per day

1927 Lockheed develops hydraulic brakes

1928 Cadillac introduces synchromesh transmission

1937 Oldsmobile offers first automatic transmission

1939 Buick introduces first flashing electric turn signals

1952 Cadillac, Oldsmobile, and Buick introduce first power steering

1965 Motor Vehicle Air Pollution Control Act is passed

1966 Ralph Nader publishes *Unsafe at Any Speed.* Manufacturers are forced to introduce safety measures

ROAD CONSTRUCTION HIGHLIGHTS

1899 First automobile garage opens in New York, and A. L. Dyke establishes first auto parts and supply business in St. Louis

1901 New York becomes first state to license automobiles and Connecticut enacts first motor vehicle law

1908 First family transcontinental trip, made in a Packard

1912 First white lines appear in the middle of streets in Redlands, California

1916 Woodrow Wilson signs Federal Aid Road Act, providing first federal money for road building

1925 Lincoln Highway (Route 30) completed, linking the east to the west

1940 Pennsylvania Turnpike, first modern U.S. long-distance road, opens

1956 Interstate Highway Act passed

The above represents only a sampling of thousands of major and minor developments relating to the automobile and the highways upon which it travels. Readers will recognize the significance of 1958 when the first Datsuns were imported into the United States, 1960 when the first Toyotas arrived, and October 1973, when the Arab oil producers imposed their first ban on exports of oil to the United States, resulting a year later in the imposition of a national fifty-five miles-per-hour speed limit to conserve fuel.

If you would like to learn more about the history of the development of the automobile, visit your nearest public library. Chances are they have several books dealing with the subject.

History of Automobilia

This is actually a two-part story—the history of automobile collecting and the history of automobile collectibles. Saving and restoring automobiles came first. Individuals involved in this process did acquire some automobilia, but always as secondary objects to enhance the presentation of their car collections.

James Melton, opera and popular-music tenor, is the most notable early automobile collector. He started collecting prior to the 1939–40 New York World's Fair. He exhibited his collection to the public. Its last exhibition site was Hypoluxo, Florida, where three-quarters of a mile was required to display all the cars Melton owned.

Other early automobile museum collections included: Long Island Automotive Museum, Southampton, New York, featuring the collection of Austin Clark, Jr.; Henry Ford Museum, Dearborn, Michigan; Swigert Memorial Motor Museum, Huntingdon, Pennsylvania; and Thompson Products Auto Museum (now the Frederick C. Crawford Auto-Aviation Museum), Cleveland, Ohio. The Henry Ford Museum, Swigert Memorial Motor Museum, and Frederick C. Crawford Auto-Aviation Museum are still open to the public.

Harrah's Automobile Collection, located in Reno, Nevada, was the most famous of all American automobile collections, housing over 1,500 different cars. Unfortunately, most of the collection was dispersed after Bill Harrah's death. The museum survives, a shadow of its former self. In 1996 the Behring Automotive Museum (3700 Blackhawk Plaza Circle, Danville, CA 94506) opened an art museum wing that features one of the largest automobilia collections in the United States.

Collectors of automobiles organized, at least in North America. Antique and vintage car collectors' clubs located outside the United States are few and far between. The Antique Automobile Club of America, Inc. (PO Box 417, Hershey, PA 17033), organized in 1935. The Horseless Carriage Club of America (128 S. Cypress Street, Orange, CA 92666) followed in 1937, a reaction to the strong eastern dominance of the AACA. The Veteran Motor Car Club of America (PO Box 360788, Strongsville, OH 44136), focusing on brass-era automobiles, also was organized prior to World War II. The Classic Car Club of America (1645 Des Plaines River Road, Ste. 7, Des Plaines, IL 60018), concentrating on cars made between 1925 and 1948, is of more recent origin.

The American Automobile Association was organized in 1902 in Chicago, when delegates from nine independent motor clubs united as a single unit. The Association had five goals: (1) enactment of liberal laws regulating the use of automobiles on public highways, (2) protection of the legal rights of users of motor vehicles, (3) support of public highways, (4) development of the automobile, and (5) equitable regulations of automobile racing and trials of endurance and efficiency. In 1904 the AAA sponsored an automobile endurance run from New York to the St. Louis World's Fair. Today the AAA has over 39 million members and lists as its purposes to provide specialized services for its members and to protect the rights, safety, comfort, and economic well-being of motorists and travelers.

Collecting automobilia owes its origins to the

numerous car shows and flea markets that sprung up across America. The Pebble Beach Concours d'Elegance (Pebble Beach, California), Meadow Brook Concours (Meadow Brook, Michigan), and Burn Foundation Concours (Lehigh University, Bethlehem, Pennsylvania) represent the high-end, invitational car show circuit.

The Hershey Car Show (Hershey, Pennsylvania), the granddaddy of the car show/flea market, is an AACA-sponsored regional event. Other major car shows and/or flea markets include: Awkscht Fescht (Macungie, Pennsylvania); three Carlisle (Pennsylvania) shows; the show accompanying the Kruse Auburn Collector Car Auction, held annually for the benefit of the Auburn-Cord-Duesenberg Museum (Auburn, Indiana); and the Iola (Wisconsin) Old Car Show & Swap Meet. The National Motor Museum, located in Beaulieu, Hampshire, sponsors the British equivalent of Hershey.

Automobile auctions of antique and classic cars also play a major role in the collecting of automobilia. Barrett-Jackson, Rick Cole Auction, and Kruse International are a few of the major auction firms. Automobile collectibles are sold as part of these and similar auctions.

The Society of Automotive Historians (PO Box 339, Matamora, PA 18336) encourages its members to do automotive research. *Automobile Quarterly* (PO Box 348, Kutztown, PA 19530) is the scholarly journal for automobile and automobilia collectors. *Mobilia* (PO Box 575, Middlebury, VT 05753), a monthly periodical, leads in reporting automobilia collecting trends in the 1990s.

No history of automobile collecting would be complete without acknowledging two major periodicals specializing in providing a market for the sale of antique, classic, and recent automobiles, automobile parts, and automobilia. *Hemming's Motor News* (PO Box 100, Bennington, VT 05201) was first published in 1951; *Old Cars* (700 East State Street, Iola, WI 54990) dates from 1971.

Finally, Transmobilia, the first show devoted exclusively to the sale of automobile and other transportation collectibles, was launched in November 1995 in Allentown, Pennsylvania. Based on the success of the first show, the promoters made a decision to make the show an annual event.

In Summary

What links the history of the automobile and the history of automobilia? The answer is the love/hate relationships involving the automobile. Many of the objects—prints, sheet music, steins, and valentines—illustrated in this book focus on the conflict between automobile lover and hater.

Fortunately, the vast majority of the objects show man's love and not hatred of the automobile. The love affair with the motorcar in the early years of the twentieth century was reflected in dozens of personal items, such as pins, shaving mugs, and toys. The appeal was universal—young and old, male and female. The farmer no longer had to hitch old Dobbin to the wagon and make a time-consuming trip to town. He got in his Model "T" and headed for the city, now just a short distance away. The automobile and the collectibles associated with it brought us closer together as a community and a nation.

We have not lost our love affair with the automobile as we approach the twenty-first century. Shows introducing new car models held in New York, Chicago, Paris, and other major centers attract large crowds. There is little doubt that these cars are tomorrow's vintage automobiles and the items associated with them tomorrow's automobilia.

However, most collectors look backward, not forward. They believe that there is far more beauty in a 1930s Cord or a late 1950s Chevrolet than today's look-alike models. And—they are right!

2.

COLLECTING TIPS

Automobile collectibles are fun. The challenge is to make and keep the act of collecting fun, too. It requires only a small step for the collector to cross over the line that separates collecting as fun from collecting that is deadly serious, highly competitive work. When collecting crosses the line and the fun disappears, there is something wrong. Collecting is about enjoyment. It should be mentally relaxing and not exhausting.

The three major value keys for automobilia are condition, scarcity, and displayability. Three additional factors that can enhance value are objects shaped like or that illustrate a specific model automobile, linked with a specific manufacturer, and/or date prior to 1930 (1915 is even better).

Condition is king in the mid-1990s. In fact, collectors have gone condition mad. Everyone wants objects, even when they are 75 to 100 years old, to be in mint condition, i.e., to look as though they just came off the assembly line. As a result, newer collectors pass on items they should acquire.

Signs of age, including very minor wear, are essential to authenticating a period piece. They add character and show that the piece was considered important enough to save. A strong argument can be made that objects made after 1975 should be collected only in mint condition. After 1975, collectors and the general public had developed a collecting consciousness. They bought mint-in-the-box items and put them away. Prior to 1975, collectors should focus on objects in fine condition; they should be complete and show no visible damage of any kind at arm's length. One can be a little more forgiving for pre-1920 objects, but completeness and an unmarred visible surface must remain the key collecting goal.

Beware of scarcity as a value key. Almost every automobile collectible was mass produced. If there is one, there are probably dozens, even hundreds. There are very few one-of-a-kind objects. The ability to judge scarcity comes only from years of experience as a collector. It is no small coincidence that scarcity increases when a person decides to sell an object he owns. Assuming the object you are examining is common is the safest buying approach. You will be right far more often than you are wrong.

Many automobile collectibles purchased in the mid-1990s are not bought to be added to someone's collection but for decorative purposes, primarily to be used by a non-collector as a decorative accent. The higher the pizzazz factor, the higher the value is the general rule. Items with strong display aesthetics and graphics command premium prices, even when relatively new.

Specialists outnumber generalists a thousand to one in the realm of automobilia. The field is vast. The only way to build a meaningful collection is to specialize. The wonderful thing about automobile collectibles is that there is no end to the number of possible avenues a collection can take. Type of object (clocks, steins, etc.), chronological time period (brass era, 1950s, etc.), automobile company (Ford, Chevrolet, etc.), region (automobile collectibles from and/or related only to York County, Pennsylvania), and body or model type (convertibles, Corvettes) are just a few approaches.

Chances are great that you will specialize in an area of automobilia that relates to your own youth. Nostalgia is a big factor in the determination of what one collects. The plus side is that your collection helps you relive your youth on a daily basis. The downside is, many of your items are "one generation" collectibles. Once the generation that grew up with them and remembers them dies, their value diminishes.

It is for this reason that investing and/or speculating in automobilia is extremely risky. There is no guarantee that an object will continue to increase in value as it becomes older. In fact, just the opposite is true. Many models of pre-1930s cars sell today for half the dollar value that these same cars brought ten to twenty years ago. The same holds true for automobilia. Brass automobile lights, once a darling among automobile collectors, are a tough sell in the mid-1990s market.

Tom Funk, editor of *Mobilia*, was asked to pick his top five automobile collectibles. He named Ayton Senna Formula 1 racing helmets (one sold in the mid-1990s for over $51,000), sales catalogs and print advertising for Pontiac's "wide track" campaign (1959–1971), B-movie hot rod and motorcycle film posters, Kellogg's NASCAR cereal boxes, and late 1960s plastic funny car model kits, such as Roger Lindamond's "Color Me Gone." In twenty years—no, in five years—a top five list will be very different. The 1990s and the first decades of the twenty-first century will be recorded in collecting history as the period of "craze collecting"—the category that is in today and is likely to be out tomorrow. Trends change quickly, sometimes in a matter of months.

What does all this mean? There is one simple answer: Collect what you like because you like it. This collecting philosophy makes you a winner. It infuses your collecting experience with a sense of adventure and excitement and makes seeking, acquiring, and displaying objects a source of continual pleasure.

Displaying Your Collection

Before you display your automobilia, you need to inventory, research, and prepare them for display. This is the part of collecting that is work, but something that needs to be done. A good inventory record tells you and your heirs where, when, from whom, and how much you paid in the process of acquiring your objects. This information will prove invaluable in the future. Take the time to do it.

Many collectors consider the time spent researching an object the most enjoyable part of collecting. Research provides an object with a history, a story that can be told repeatedly to those who ask. While automobile collectibles are inanimate objects, research makes them come alive. Many collectors, especially those with an investment mentality, never experience the joys involved with accurately identifying, dating, and assigning an object to its proper historic, social, and economic context. Such individuals miss the real joy of collecting.

Today most automobile collectibles are cleaned and ready for immediate display when they are sold. Restoration and conservation are rarely required by purchasers, having already been done by the seller. Yet do not overlook objects whose only flaw is that they are dirty. A few minutes with the appropriate cleaning material can turn a dirty peasant into a crown prince.

Know your restoration abilities. Many collectors have ruined objects when attempting to do cleaning and repairs for which they lack the appropriate skills. When in doubt, take your objects to a specialist.

One of the factors that determines what you collect is the amount of space you have available to display and store the automobilia you acquire. If you live in an apartment, it is highly unlikely that you will collect gasoline pumps or full-size automobiles.

The good news is that many three-dimensional automobile collectibles fall into the "smalls" category, like inkwells, pocket watches, etc. Further, the number of paper categories is vast, and 10,000 postcards fit nicely into two file cabinets.

When displaying your objects, make your primary goal to not destroy the objects through display. Do not glue paper to matting materials; keep paper out of contact with direct sunlight. Make certain that the shelves that hold your ceramic and glass collectibles are properly secured to the walls or that the curio cabinet is properly balanced so it will not tip over. Provide easy access to objects you are most likely to handle when visitors come. Many collectors have broken prized pieces by knocking them over while trying to pick up an object located on the back of a shelf.

Change your displays often. Collectors have a tendency to put objects in one location and leave them there forever. There is no fun in that. Moving your objects on a regular basis means visiting with them on a regular basis. You will be surprised how often you discover something about the object that you failed to notice in the past.

Keep in mind that as a collector, you are only a custodian for the objects in your collection. Someday they will give pleasure to another collector. Adopt the Boy Scout approach of always leaving something in better shape than you found it.

Do not let the collection own you. Some people cut short their vacations because they worry about the security of their collection. They have sleepless nights concerned that someone might break into their home and steal part of their collection. Invest in a professional fire and theft security system and acquire adequate insurance through a fine arts rider to your household policy.

Finally, never lose sight of the goal that introduced this chapter—fun. If collecting stops being fun, it is time to re-examine your priorities. Make certain your collecting always moves ahead on the right side of the road.

3.

STATE-OF-THE-MARKET REPORT

The collecting of automobilia is one of the most rapidly growing collecting categories in the mid-1990s. It's hot and getting hotter. It has divorced itself from collecting the cars themselves and evolved as a collecting category in its own right.

Automobile collecting began in earnest after World War II. Initially, the focus was on cars from the brass and gas era, i.e., cars with brass radiators and gaslit headlamps. Material such as repair manuals, catalogs, and advertising items were collected primarily for research and to enhance a car's display. Rarely was this material collected for its own sake. Further, individuals tended to collect only the secondary material that related to the car or cars they owned.

This has totally changed in the 1990s. Many contemporary collectors of automobilia do not even own an antique or classic car. Those who do prefer cars that can be driven on today's superhighways as opposed to showcase cars that must be trailed from show to show. This trend is important because money collectors previously spent on the restoration of older automobiles now is being channeled to automobilia. This shift in collecting emphasis also is evident in the current downward price spiral for common antique automobiles.

Automobile collectors have significantly changed their focus during the past ten years. The market for automobilia from 1910 to 1950 is soft. Many are concerned that it will never recycle again. There are some exceptions, such as high-ticket automobiles like the Pierce Arrow and collectibles with strong design and aesthetics. Automobiles and automobilia from the 1950s through the 1970s are where the action is in today's market. One reason is that collectors who identify with antique automobiles are dying and not being replaced by younger collectors who care about these cars. The current crop of collectors looks more to their own generation for collecting inspiration and not to the era of their parents, grandparents, and great-grandparents.

Automobilia came into its own in the late 1970s and early 1980s. The market is now twenty-five years old—mature, but still with a great deal of youthful enthusiasm. Contrasting those automobilia categories that were hot in 1987 with those that are hot in 1997 demonstrates the continuing evolution of the market.

HOT IN 1987	HOT IN 1997
Advertising	Advertising
Automobile accessories, brass	Games and puzzles
Ceramic collectibles	Gasoline station collectibles
Holiday items with an auto theme	License plates
License plates	Pedal cars
Mascots	Postcards, especially real photo cards
Pinback buttons and badges	Racing collectibles
Toys, dominated by cast iron	Toys, dominated by sheet steel, post–World War II Japanese tin, and Ertl

A few automobilia categories, such as advertising and license plates, have stood the test of time. Others have enjoyed a brief five- to ten-year collecting craze and then softened or virtually disappeared. Look for the market to continue to shift its emphasis in the years ahead. Trendiness is a major aspect of today's collecting market.

It is time to classify gasoline station collectibles as a separate category. Previously, gasoline pumps and advertising signs were purchased to serve as props to enhance the display presentation of a car. Large blocks of gasoline station collectibles, such as uniforms and maps, were ignored. No longer. Today gasoline station collectibles have a strong support structure in place—specialized shows, collectors' clubs, periodicals, and numerous reference books and price guides. Anything gasoline station–related is collectible.

Crossover collecting has always played a major role in automobilia. Initially, advertising collectors drove up the price on premier automobile advertising pieces, especially those with great graphics. Today, advertising character collectors, paper collectors of all types, ceramic and glass collectors, etc., actively seek automobilia that relates to their specialties, often paying far more for an object than the collector of automobilia.

Should collectors of toy vehicles be classified as automobile collectors or toy collectors? The answer is both. Toy vehicles, even those that are generic, have always been part of the automobilia market. It is impossible to go to an automobile flea market or show without finding toys. In the

1990s toys provide a viable alternative to collecting the "big" cars. You can assemble a fleet of Ford Thunderbird promotional models, toys, and plastic model kits at less cost than buying a single full-size classic example.

The shifting collecting focus in the toy sector parallels that in the general automobilia market. The era of the cast-iron toy collector is ending. Pressed steel toys from the 1930s through the 1950s currently are king of the hill. However, plastic toys of the post–World War II period are coming on strong. Look for them to dominate the scene in the twenty-first century.

The future for automobilia is extremely bright. As long as there is a love affair with the automobile, there will always be an automobilia market. This aside, the building blocks that have been put in place over the past decades to support the automobilia market are more than adequate to ensure its continued growth.

Dozens of books dealing with automobilia have been published during the past decade. Specialized automobilia shows have developed. In 1995 I helped found the Transmobilia Show, held annually the first weekend in November in Allentown, Pennsylvania. The role played by automobilia at car, paper, and toy shows continues to grow.

Several periodicals now focus on automobilia. *Automobile Quarterly* is the granddaddy of the bunch. However, credit *Mobilia* with raising interest in automobilia to a new height. It appeals to the new, young generation of collectors. Check out *Mobilia*'s website at www.mobilia.com. Articles about automobilia appear regularly in general antiques and collectibles trade papers—the more press, the more interest.

Any state-of-the-market report would be incomplete if it did not discuss the role of foreign collectors. In the late 1990s automobilia is an international market. The Dutch, English, French, and Germans are in North America buying back the automobilia American collectors purchased in Europe immediately following World War II. For the moment, they are ignoring American material, much to the delight of American collectors. The Japanese remain minor players in the overall American market. However, they are major buyers of Japanese lithograph tin toy cars from the post–World War II period.

4.

AUTOMOBILE ACCESSORIES

Auto accessories fall into two categories:

1. **period equipment used in and associated with the manufacturing of the automobile and**
2. **additional objects to be applied to the car or used in conjunction with the car.**

Fortunately for the motorist, hobbyist, and restorer, many of the brass lamps and horns survived the scrap drives associated with World War I, World War II, and the Korean War.

My collecting interest always has been focused on the early period of the development of the automobile. Therefore, most of the items pictured are oil or gas, i.e., acetylene fueled. Many of the horns are brass—the larger the automobile, the larger the horn.

Clocks

■

Clock, dash, Jager Watch Company, Swiss works, $75–100.

(Left) clock, dash, Keyless Auto Clock, rim wind and rim set, marked "Made in the U.S.A.," $75–100; *(right)* clock, dash, brass, made in Boston, Massachusetts, key wind, $75–100.

Clock, dash, Oldsmobile, rim wind, eight day, $100–150.

Clock, dash, M.A. Smiths, spring wound, face opens like a door, $75–100.

Hubcaps

■

Although some hubcaps are unmarked, most feature either the first letter of the automobile manufacturer or the name of the automobile. Since there are over 1,500 different car companies in the United States, it is possible to assemble a major collection of hubcaps. When possible, avoid buying a hubcap that is damaged.

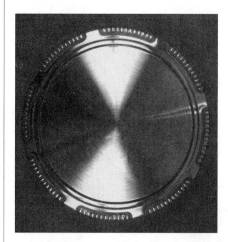

Hubcap, Dodge Polara, 1973, spun aluminum, 9" diameter, $8–10.

Hubcaps. *(Left)* Paige, brass, $15–20; *(right)* E. R. Thomas Company, "Thomas Flyer," cast brass, circa 1909, $100–150.

Hubcaps. *(Upper left)* Buick, spun aluminum, $20–25. *(Center)* Ford Model "T," nickel-plated brass, used after the brass era of cars, $15–25. *(Upper right)* Peerless, spun aluminum, $20–25.

Lights

■

Light, side, Stay-Lit-Brass Light Bail light, Atwood Manufacturing Company, Amesbury, Massachusetts, 14" to top of bail, circa 1908, $200–225.

Light, side, Corcoran Brass Light, Corcoran Brass Company, Cincinnati, Ohio, 13" high, $200–225.

Light, side, Atwood Model 53, Atwood Manufacturing Company, Amesbury, Massachusetts, 13 1/8" high, $200–225.

Light, side, Solar Model 41, patented December 8, 1903, brass, 13 1/2" high, $175–200.

Lights, side pair, Solar Model 41, patented December 8, 1903, brass, 3 1/2" high, $350–400 for pair.

Lights, side, pair, Solar Model 933, patented 1909, brass, $250–300 for pair.

Lights, side, pair, made by Gray and Davis for Cadillac, brass nickel plated, circa 1918, $125–175 for pair.

Light, side, for use on electric car, brass and black painted metal, $65–85.

Mascot, boy with toy auto, French, brass, circa 1930s, $75–90. This same figure was also used for bookends.

Light, side, left and right view of Never Out Safety Lamps for carriages and early horseless carriages, $75–100 each.

Mascot, eagle, Chenard et Walcker, polished pewter, 1907, $100–125.

Mascot, Ford Model "T," standard brass radiator cap, 1913, $15–20.

Mascots

Early radiator caps were utilitarian. As the years passed, the radiator cap began serving a dual purpose—a cap for the radiator and a decorative element for the hood of the car.

Mascots, also known as hood ornaments, added a personal touch to one's automobile, a predecessor of today's vanity license plate. There are three major types of radiator mascots: (1) company logo, (2) custom made, and (3) fantasy.

Many mascots were lost over the years as cars were scrapped. It takes time to assemble a substantial collection. There is always a special thrill when a previously unknown mascot appears at auction or, even better, a garage sale.

Mascot, Ford Model "T," homemade radiator applied to top of standard cap, probably advertisement for radiator repair shop truck, brass nickel plated, circa 1920, $50–60.

Mascot, Franklin, Series 11, "Aura Vincit" (Air Conquers), 1925–1928, made by Sterling Bronze Company, designed by G. Derujinky, $25–30. Franklin automobiles were air cooled.

Mascot, Mack, brass, circa 1914, $35–40.

Mascot, Horlocker Company, penguin with "H" on breast, custom made, 1920s, $200–250. Horlocker was an Allentown, Pennsylvania, brewery.

Mascot, Mathis, "Eternal Flame," chrome plated zinc casting, 1928, $75–100.

Mascot, Mack, bulldog, collar marked "Mack," patented 1932, $50–60.

Mascot, Oakland, 1928 Eagle, manufactured by Ternsted Manufacturing Company, designed by William Schnell, nickel plated zinc casting, $65–85.

Mascot, peacock, Villars, France, thermometer on back of casting, circa 1920s, $75–90.

Mascot, Pontiac, nickel and copper plated cast zinc, 1927, $25–30.

Mascot, auto ascending from clouds, marked "Verecke, France," circa 1920s, $75–90.

Mascot, unknown manufacturer, motorist with goggles, designed by Jean Verschneider, brass, 4 3/4" high, circa 1915, $150–175.

Mascot, unknown manufacturer, motorist indicating speed, designed by Jean Verschneider, brass, 6" high, $150–175.

Mascot, unknown manufacturer, motorist with bulb horn, designed by Jean Verschneider, brass, 5" high, $150–175.

Mascot, Willy-Knight, Knight's helmet on wings, chrome plated zinc casting, circa 1924, $25–30.

Miscellaneous

Advertising, figurine, Michelin Man, Mr. Bibidum, plastic, white, 8" wide, 12" tall, 1981, $35.

Auto Ice Raft, Haring Company, aid for freeing car from snow or ice, $100.

Advertising, promotional model, plastic, Chrysler, 1963, two-door hardtop sedan, cypress tan color, 8 1/4" long, 3 3/4" wide, 2 1/4" high, period packaging, information on end flap, showroom promotion, $150.

Mirror, spare tire rearview, Yankee Mirroscope Company, $200–225.

Advertising, promotional model, plastic, 1963 Ford Galaxie convertible, champagne color, 8 1/4" long, 3 3/8" wide, period packaging, mailed by company, $150.

Oil purifier, Standard Electro-Magnet Oil De Carbonizer, $100–150. Pour old oil in the top spout, turn on the battery, and out comes purified oil from the bottom.

Pump, tire, Peerless, Peerless Accessories Manufacturing Company, Chicago, Illinois, 4-cylinder, $75–100.

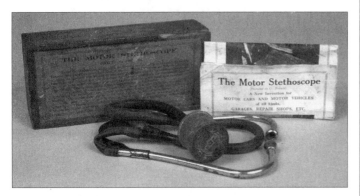

Stethoscope, English, used to hear motor noises, $200–250.

Wheel lock, Auto Theft Signal System, Miller Chapman Company, Los Angeles, California, patented 1914, $100–125.

License Plate, Pennsylvania, 1958 with applied stickers through 1964, blue ground, yellow border and letters/numbers, 12" x 6", $3–5.

Warning Devices

Horn, exhaust, Aermore, Fulton Company, Milwaukee, Wisconsin, $100.

Horn, Nonpariel, brass, 3-coil, 12 1/2", $250–300.

Horn, Rubes, brass, bulb, patented 1909, $125.

Horn, Rubes, brass, bulb, Model "T" Ford, circa 1911, $150.

5.

CERAMICS AND GLASS

It did not take ceramic artists and manufacturers long to realize that the automobile presented a natural subject for their wares. They were motivated by a number of considerations. The speed and power represented by the horseless carriage was the initial attraction. However, the problems associated with that speed and power soon became the subject of serious and comic pieces depicting events associated with the vehicle and those who operated it.

The vast majority of early ceramic automobilia—items made before 1940—is English or Continental in origin. Quality varied, from highly aesthetic bronzes to novelty bisque figurines serving as carnival and fair souvenirs.

As the automobile became more sophisticated, so did its portrayal. Early items featured generic cars; later works depicted specific makes.

Shaving mugs, steins, and tobacco jars featuring automobile images are three of the most popular forms desired by collectors. All three are pricey categories. Those with a limited budget are advised to consider bisque novelty figurines, many of which sell for under $100.

Glass items, with the exception of those used as accessories for the car, like auto vases, are scarce. Hand painting or engraving glass was expensive. Glass also broke. As a result, glass items bring premium prices.

Ceramics

Ashtray, Austria, bisque, shape of rhinoceros dressed in driving togs, duster, cap, and glasses, hand painted, 5 3/8" x 6 7/8", circa 1910, $250–300.

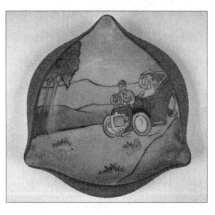

Ashtray, Nippon, hand painted, 5 1/2" tip to tip, circa 1905, $200–250.

Bottle, bisque, German, 5 1/4" x 2 1/2", circa 1905, $50–75.

Box, pin, bisque, Easter rabbits, eggs in hood of car, 3 1/4" x 4 1/4", circa 1910, $100–125.

Clock, Austria, A. Forster Company, depicts 120 hp Mercedes racing car designed by Rornig, electrical headlights and digital paper clock, 10 3/4" x 22 3/8", circa 1908, $6,000–7,000. I purchased this clock many years ago. It was used in a window display at a Kinney shoe store.

Condiment Set, French, pig driver, $125–150. Possibly an early depiction of the "road hog," a much condemned driver type.

Cookie Jar, French, white body with black trim, body of chauffeur and backseat are removable lid, 7 3/8" x 13 1/2", circa 1910, $400–600.

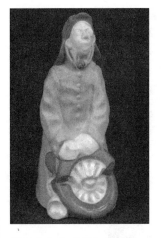

Figurine, Austrian, chauffeur, 4" wide, 9" high, circa 1910, one of pair, $350–400.

Figurine, Austrian, female, wearing duster and veil, 5 1/8" wide, 9" high, circa 1910, one of pair, $350–400.

Cup and Saucer, Nippon, circa 1905, $75–100.

Figurine, French, bisque, chauffeur, marked "Puff Puff," 2 1/4" wide, 7 5/8" high, circa 1910, $150–200.

Figurines, pair, German, bisque, male and female chauffeurs, 3" wide, 9 1/4" high, circa 1910, $300–350 pair. Note impressed image of early car at bottom of each figure.

Egg Cup, French, G. LeGesch, blue underglaze, sold as a souvenir at the 1896 Paris to Trouville race held in August 1896, 4 1/4" wide, 4 3/8" high, $250–300.

Figurine, Italian, pottery, chauffeur, high glaze, 3" wide, 8" high, $75–100.

Egg Cup, French, angel driving the car, 3 1/2" wide, 2 1/2" high, $100–125. Many early egg cup souvenirs of this type featured the devil driving an automobile.

Flask, German, Schaffer Vader, "Puff Puff," 2 3/4" x 5 1/2", circa 1906, $350–500.

Reverse.

Match Holder, German, bisque, chauffeur's head, 2" wide, 3 1/4" high, $500–750. This is the same motif as found in the tobacco jar (humidor) made by Ernst Bohne Sôhne Company.

Mug, half-liter, German, pottery, "For the City of Detroit, 'The Automobile City,' " circa 1910, $75–100.

Mustard Jar, 2 3/4" wide, 4" high, circa 1905, $50–60.

Nodder, bisque, chauffeur holding money purse and dead duck, poised to pay farmer, 3 1/4" wide, 7 1/4" high, $300–350. The red nose indicates he is a drinker and an irresponsible driver.

Figure Jar (left), head and shoulders lift up, $100–125. Nodder (right), French, chauffeur (male), 2 1/2" wide, 4 1/2" high, circa 1910, $150–200.

Nodders, German, bisque, chauffeurs (female and male), 2 7/8" wide, 5 5/8" high, circa 1910, marked "9677," $350–400 for the pair.

Novelty, German, bisque, corn cob car with Black driver and passenger, 4 1/4" wide, 3" high, circa 1910, $175–200.

Novelty, German, you decide if it's a baby or lady driver, circa 1910, $35–40.

Novelty, German, car, green in color, 3 3/8" wide, 2 3/4" high, circa 1905, $65–75.

Perfume Atomizer, French, Aladdin Company of Paris, electric lamp heats the porcelain which vaporizes the perfume; lamps also illuminate driver's and mechanic's coats, 4 3/8" x 11 1/4", circa 1925, $900–1,000.

Novelty, German, bisque, auto with dog in backseat, circa 1905, $65–75.

Pin Cushion, German, seated child driver, figure measures 2 1/2" high, $125–150.

Novelty, German, bisque, car with female driver, head moves, 5 3/4" wide, 4 1/2" high, circa 1905, $65–75.

Pipe, carved meerschaum, Baby PANHARD, folding stem to enable pipe to be carried in pocket, 2 1/4" x 5", circa 1900, $300–350.

Novelty, German, bisque, pig driver, 6 1/2" wide, 5 1/2" high, circa 1905, $250–300.

Pipe, carved meerschaum, automobile part of the bowl, 7" x 2 1/4", circa 1910, $400–450.

Pipe, carved meerschaum, car with driver and female passenger, 6" x 2", circa 1903, $400–450.

Pitcher, Buffalo Pottery Company, Buffalo, New York, motif featuring Roosevelt Teddy Bears, "The Roosevelt Bears take an Auto Ride. / We've broken something, said TEDDY -G. / It's underneath, get down and see," copyright Edward Stern Company, 4 1/2" wide, 8" high, 1907, $450–500.

Pitcher, German, woman driver carrying "Benzin" can, marked "Æ Gesetzlich geschützt," 11" x 6 1/4", circa 1908, $550–600.

Pitcher, German, chauffeur, marked "Benzin" in mold, imprinted above the glaze "Souvenir of Coney Island," 3 3/4" wide, 6 1/2" high, circa 1910, $150–200.

Plate, 10 1/2" diameter, French, blue tone, $110–125. Designed to be hung.

Plate, French, luncheon, one of Terre de Fer set, titled "Car in Tow," $20–25.

Plate, 10 1/2" diameter, French, luncheon, one of Terre de Fer set, pictures horse frightened by car, $20–25.

Plate, 8 5/8" diameter, French, titled "Killing Machine" (a subject often used in early automobile objets d'art), circa 1905, $75–100. Designed to be hung.

Plate, German, Villeroy & Boch, Mettlach, $200–250.

Biscuit Jar, "A Horse A Horse," 9 3/4" wide, 9 1/8" high, $250–300.

Roseville Pottery Company's Tourist Series, Roseville Pottery Company, Zanesville, Ohio, produced between 1906 and 1916. Cream-colored ground with hand-painted transfer print. Twenty-nine different objects made.

Jardiniere, 9" wide, 10" high, $850–900.

(Left) Pitcher, "Room for One," 4 1/8" wide, 6 5/8" high, $150–175. *(Right)* Mug, "Blood Money," 4 1/8" wide, 5 7/8" high, $100–125.

Vase, lady driver, 7" high, 5" wide, circa 1915, $850–900.

Plate, 10 1/2" diameter, "Blood Money," $125–150.

Plate, 10 1/2" diameter, "Deaf," $125–150.

Royal Doulton's Motorist Series, Royal Doulton China, designed by George Holdcroft for Royal Doulton, produced between 1903 and 1913, total of eight different scenes; same scene can be found on different forms.

Plate, 10 1/2" diameter, "Itch Yer on Guvenor?," $125–150.

Salt and Pepper, three-piece set, car holder, Japan, circa 1930s, $75–100.

Plate, 10 1/2" diameter, "Nerve Tonic," $125–150.

Blank mugs were made in Austria and France and sent to the United States for decoration. The patron of the barber shop would order a special design based on his customer's occupation, fraternal group, or special preferences. The auto enthusiast often had his favorite car pictured on his mug.

Shaving Mug, W. Copewid, marked "Limoges, France/T & V," shows early car, but dated 1922, $250–300.

Plate, 10 1/2" diameter, "Room for One," $125–150.

Shaving Mug, T.S.G., marked "Vienna, Austria," gray race-about, A. Riedel artist, circa 1910, $750–800.

Plate, 10 1/2" diameter, untitled, $125–150.

Shaving Mug, Patterson, marked "Austria/W," Franklin type hooded car, circa 1910, $225–250.

Shaving Mug, Sullivan, marked "Limoges, France/T & V," red touring car, $225–250.

Shaving Mug, German, black roadster, circa 1915, $225–250.

Stein, Mettlach, DAC, made for German Automobile Club, circa 1910, $1,200–1,500.

Steins. *(right)* German, Munchen Transportation Show, 1911, $350–400; *(left)* German Auto Club, 1/2 liter, $450–500.

Stein, German, E. Bohne Söhne, race driver, circa 1910, 3 7/8" wide, 6" high, $1,000–1,200.

Stein, German, reproduction of E. Bohne Sôhne race driver stein, same mold, but coloring changed to avoid confusion with period piece, $250–300.

Stein, German, 1/2 liter, Number 1537, .5 liter, circa 1905, $850–900. Auto has just run over chicken.

Stein, German, souvenir, "Niagara Falls, Canada," circa 1910, $850–900. Auto has just run over duck.

Stein, German, 1/2 liter, Number 1513, speeding auto, policeman writing a ticket, circa 1910, $850–900.

Teapot, English (Sadler, Ltd., circa 1927) and American (Superior Quality Kitchenware Company, between 1927 and mid-1930s), 4 1/4" x 8 1/2", $450–500. Trailer serves as jelly jar.

Stein, German, 1/2 liter, marked "Geschutzt," motorcycle motif, $1,400–1,500.

Tobacco Jar, German, high glaze, 6" x 7", $300–350.

Tobacco Jar, Austrian, 5" wide, 6 1/2" high, circa 1915, $250–300.

Stein, German, 2 liter, auto's driver asks directions, circa 1910, $450–500.

Tobacco Jar, German, high glaze, marked "W 5+5"/Number 3338," $200–250.

Tobacco Jar, bisque, designed by artist T.S., found in both high glaze and matte finish, 4 1/2" wide, 5 3/8" high, $125–150.

Tobacco Jar, Japanese, Nippon, hand painted, circa 1910, $450–500.

Tobacco Jars. *(Left)* Round chauffeur (almost egg shaped), $175–200; *(right)* Peko figure, German comic, as chauffeur, 4 1/4" wide, 5 3/8" high, circa 1920s, $125–150.

Tobacco Jar, Japanese, Nippon China Humidor, circa 1905, hand-painted scenes, stained ground, design to resemble a leather sewn cover, 4 3/4" wide, 7 1/8" high, circa 1905, $550–600.

Tobacco Jar, German, listed in Ernst Bohne Sôhne Company catalog as "Chauffeur/Race Driver," 3 1/2" wide, 5 1/2" high, $1,750–2,000. Image also used for match holder and pipe.

Vase, V. Gilliard, made for MOTOBLOC Company for display at 1907 automobile show in Paris, 12" wide, 19" high, $4,500–5,000.

Tobacco Jar, German, dog driving, 7 1/8" wide, 4 1/2" high, circa 1910, $175–200.

Vase, French, bisque, commemorates first automobile race, 1895 Paris to Bordeaux, 8 1/8" wide, 4 1/4" high, $450–500.

Vase, Austrian, butterfly serves as engine, cupid at wheel, body pink with green trim, circa 1905, 20" x 11 1/4" $3,500–4,000.

Vase, German, lady driving, child as footman, white porcelain, flowers painted on the body, circa 1900, $650–750.

Glass

■

Auto Vase, pressed glass, $75–100.

Auto Vase, pressed glass, etched floral design, $75–100.

Auto Vase, pressed glass, etched floral design, $75–100.

Candy Container, U. S. Glass, Miss Liberty, pressed, clear, 5 3/4" wide, 5 5/8" high, pre-1919, $450–500.

Candy Container, U.S. Glass, Stanley Steamer, pressed, clear, driver's head and body of car one casting, glass wheels with glass axles, $450–500. Designed after Frank Marriott's steamer, which was timed at 127.66 mph in 1906.

Decanter, French, hand-painted automobile and aircraft, 3 1/4" wide, 8 7/8" high, circa 1910, $100–125.

Novelty, milk glass automobile, painted red, souvenir of "New Tripoli," 4 5/8" wide, 2 1/8" high, $35–40.

Plate, pictures early Marklin toy touring car, contemporary, $50–60.

Drinking Glasses, set of five, English, hand painted, circa 1910, $75–85 per glass.

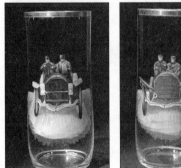

Glass, water, German, Toff/Toff, hand painted, $275–300. Painted by Mustersokutz, who also painted German steins.

Stein, automobile motif, hand painted, circa 1910, $400–450.

Wine Glass, automobile motif, hand painted, circa 1910, $150–200.

6.

METALS

It is difficult to understand in the 1990s the enormous impact the automobile had on people's everyday lives. Society became mobile. In the early years, if you owned a car, you had money.

There were many ways to flaunt car ownership and/or auto enthusiasm besides pointing to a vehicle. The automobile became a popular decorative image on a wide range of material—buttons, clocks, pocket knives, pocket watches, etc. Many of these items had a low initial cost that fell well within the means of the average consumer.

This is true even today. Several automobilia metal categories, such as pocket knives shaped as an automobile or with an automobile image, are available to the collector whose budget is in the $25 to $75 range.

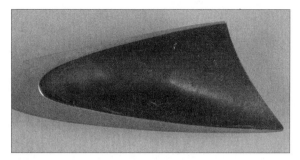

Ashtray, Chrysler, brass, logo, 1960s, black painted body, 5 3/4" long, 2" wide, $65–75.

Bronze, French, 1903 Mors race car, rubber tires, 4" wide, 1 5/8" high, $450–500. Note hand crank and chain drive.

Bronze, Austrian, hand painted, features frog driver, wire wheels with rubber tires, 2 1/4" wide, 2 1/2" high, circa 1905, $350–400.

Bronze, Austrian, features mechanic under car, 4 3/4" wide, 2 1/2" high, $450–500.

Bronze, Austrian, driver fixing flat tire while sitting on a road marker, 3" wide, 3 1/4" high, circa 1910, $350–400.

Bronze, French, Race of Death, marked "P. Mopeau/Vauthiet," period casting in two parts (car and driver separate), 6 3/4" wide, 3 1/2" high, circa 1903, $450–500. Commemorates the 1903 Paris to Madrid race. Driver is removable in period piece; reproduction is single cast with driver attached to car.

Bronze, French, Renault, hand painted, features driver and female passenger, moveable wheels, 5 5/8" wide, 2 1/8" high, circa 1930s, $125–150.

Bronze, Austrian, Touring Car, features driver and two passengers, 4" wide, 2 1/2" high, electrified servant's bell, $450–500.

Child's Cup, sterling silver, Spanish, maker unknown, Mutt and Jeff, 4" high, $180–200.

Cigar Cutter, metal wheels, wood body, 3 1/2" wide, 2 3/4" high, $275–300. The steering wheel is pushed down as a cutter bar.

Cigarette Case/Music Box, German, back lifts up to provide space for cigarettes, circa 1910, $550–600.

Cigarette Lighter, brass-plated cast white metal, hood ornament comes out as striker, 7 1/4" wide, 3 1/2" high, circa 1910, $275–300.

Clock, brass, shaped as headlamp, advertisement for Saxon lamps, 6" diameter, $450–500.

Clock, probably Austrian, cast brass, 1904-type automobile with two passengers, face of clock features wheel with wing motif, similar motif in casting, 7" wide, 6 1/4" high, $350–400.

Clock, pot metal, car under arch, arch frame holds clock, 5 1/2" wide, 10" high, $350–400.

Clock, brass and nickel-plated brass, clock in rear compartment of car, 8 3/4" wide, 3 3/4" high, circa 1910, $550–600.

Desk Set, silver-plated cast metal, Loraine Dietrich racing car, inkwell and stamp receiver, 14" wide, 5" high, circa 1908, $900–1,000.

Desk Set, cast metal with bronze wash, Mercedes, inkwell, stamp receiver, and tray for pens, 16" wide, 6 1/2" high, $900–1,000.

Filigree Car, 2 3/4" wide, 1 1/4" high, circa 1905, $200–250.

Filigree Car, 4 1/8" wide, 2 3/8" high, circa 1905, $200–250.

Inkwell, pot metal ink, 5 1/4" wide, 3 1/8" high, circa 1905, $300–350.

Filigree Car, Italian, soldered silver and gold wire, fine wires twisted and braided, 2 1/8" wide, 1 3/4" high, circa 1905, $200–250.

Place Card Holders, pair, English, silver and enamel, features a Renault-type green car with red seats and white tires, circa 1902, $100 each.

Place Card Holders, set of eight (four shown), English, silver, features car with driver and four passengers, 1 1/4" wide, 1 1/2" high, circa 1905, $90 each.

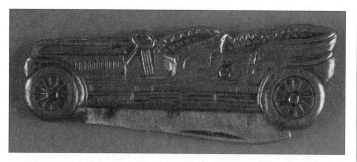

Pocket Knife, German, brass, touring car without driver, circa 1910, $40–50.

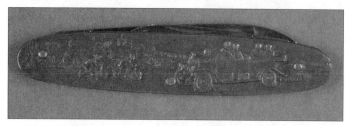

Pocket Knife, German, brass, touring car, marked "Coursulie" on spare tire, 2 1/2" long, $40–50.

Pocket Knife, obverse is 1922 Grand Prix race car, reverse is 1920s car and two bicycle riders, 3 1/2" long, $65–75. This is a reproduction marked "Made in Germany" with a Winchester blade.

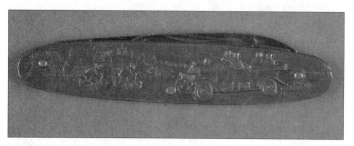

Reverse

Obverse

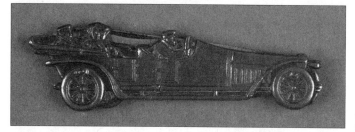

Pocket Knife, German, German silver, touring car with driver and two passengers, 2 1/2" long, circa 1920s, $45–50.

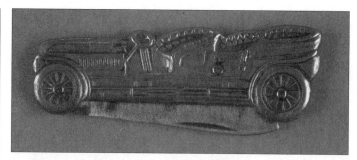

Pocket Knife, German, Layfeyette Cutlery Company, German silver, open touring car, 2 1/4" long, circa 1920, $45–50.

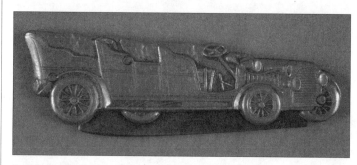

Pocket Knife, German, marked "D. Peres/ Solingen, Germany," German silver, three-seat touring car, 2 1/2" long, circa 1920s, $45–50.

Salt and Pepper Shaker Set, English, sterling silver, 3 1/2" high, circa 1910, $450–500 pair.

Tape Measure, 2 1/2" wide, 1 5/8" high, circa 1905, $75–100. Turn wheel and tape retracts.

Watch, carriage, Swiss, "Automobile Regulateur," pictures 1898-type horseless carriage on face, 2 3/4" diameter, $275–300.

Watch, carriage, silver and black enamel, case marked "Depose Argentan," car and floral decoration exposed silver, 2 3/4" diameter, circa 1905, $275–300.

Watch, carriage, Swiss mechanism and case, car in heavy relief silver, 2 3/4" diameter, circa 1905, $275–300.

Watch, pocket, silver case, relief of powered three-wheeled vehicle with driver sitting in back and two passengers (woman and child) in front, car image reminiscent of Dion-Bouton, 2" diameter, circa 1900, $275–300.

Watch, pocket, silver case, relief of farm scene with automobile with small wheels in front and larger wheels in back, driver and three passengers, two of the passengers face backward as in horse-drawn hunting carts, 2" diameter, circa 1900, $300–350.

Watch, pocket, Swiss, silver case, relief of two-seat runabout, driver and passenger, bridge with train in background, 1 3/4" diameter, circa 1900, $275–300.

Watch, pocket, Swiss, eight-day, plated (heat treated) case with dark, black finish, relief of touring car with driver and two passengers, man standing on side of road talking to passengers, marked "Louisine" on face, 2" diameter, circa 1910, $350–400.

Watch, pocket, Swiss, silver case, relief of 1900 automobile with driver and passenger, 2" diameter, $275–300.

Watch holder, nickel-plated sheet metal, rubber tires, $350–400. Radiator shell opens to offer place to hang watch.

7.

PINBACKS, DRIVING CLUB BADGES, AND STICKPINS

Celluloid pinback buttons were an inexpensive form of advertising. There are thousands of examples. While still affordable, $15 is a basic starting price. High-end buttons—those with exceptionally strong graphics, from short-lived automobile manufacturers, and of great scarcity—can sell in the mid-hundreds of dollars.

Enamel pinback buttons, generally of higher quality than celluloid ones, were worn by salesmen and given to select customers. Because they were produced in smaller quantities, they are a bit more difficult to find.

Automobile clubs around the world issued driving club badges, usually to be mounted on a car's radiator or grill. These badges conveyed a sense of belonging to an automobile fraternity.

Early drivers often wore linen dusters. It was a logical step to design fancy buttons for those dusters with an automobile theme. It is believed that most fancy button dusters were for women passengers. Duster buttons come in a wide variety of sizes and materials, e.g. hard rubber, enameled brass, tin, etc.

Buttons

■

Button, duster, unknown maker, brass, oval, woman driving circa 1905 car, 1 3/4" x 2 3/4", $75.

Button, duster, unknown maker, brass, round, race driver, 2 1/2" diameter, $75.

Button, duster, unknown maker, brass and fabric, round, image of female driver in center of wheel, 2" diameter, $100.

Driving Club Badges

■

Driving Club Badge, Auto Automobile du Cinéma, brass and enamel, film sprocket shape, 3 1/4" diameter, $35.

Driving Club Badge, Touring Club de France, white metal and enamel, 3" diameter, $45.

Driving Club Badge, Automobile and Touring Association of Israel, cast brass and enamel, 3 1/4" wide, 4 1/2" high, $75.

Driving Club Badge, Automobile Club of Marocain, white metal and enamel, 2 1/4" diameter, $65.

Patch, cloth, woven, American Racing Drivers Club, oval, white letters, red ground, yellow secondary ground behind midget race car, 4 5/8" x 2 7/8", $15–20.

Driving Club Badge, Automobile Club Martiniquais, brass and enamel, 2 1/2" diameter, $50.

Patch, cloth, woven, Automobile Association of America, 1950, oval, Official Timer Midget Racing, red on white, 5" x 3 1/4", $15–20.

Driving Club Badge, Automobile Club Torino, white metal and enamel, 2 1/4" wide, 2 1/2" high, $50.

Pinback Buttons

■

Pinback Buttons: *(top)* American Locomotive Motor Car, celluloid, National Equipment Co., 7/8" diameter, $35; *(bottom left)* American Scout, celluloid, 1 1/4" diameter, $65; *(bottom right)* American Six, celluloid, Bastian Bros., 7/8" diameter, $35.

Pinback Button, Brownie Kar, celluloid, Bastian Bros., 1 1/4" diameter, $100.

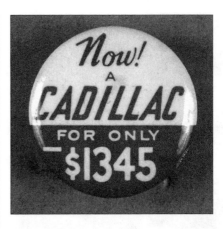

Pinback Button, Now! A Cadillac for Only $1,345, celluloid, BBCO, 1" diameter, $35.

Pinback Buttons: *(upper left)* Buick-Losey Co., celluloid, 7/8" diameter, $65; *(upper right)* Buick: Simplicity–Durability Power, celluloid, 1" diameter, $65; *(bottom)* Buick, brass and enamel, 1 1/8" diameter, $100.

Pinback Buttons: *(left)* Chevrolet Fleetline Bodies, lithograph tin, 3/4" diameter, $35; *(center top)* C-Day Is Coming, lithograph tin, L. J. Imber Co., 7/8" diameter, $35; *(center bottom)* Keep Your Eye on Chevrolet, lithograph tin, Geraghty and Co., 7/8" diameter, $35; *(right)* Watch the Leader, lithograph tin, Geraghty and Co., 7/8" diameter, $35.

Pinback Buttons: *(left)* Buick Valve in Head, celluloid, 7/8" diameter, $35; *(center)* Buick, Everybody Knows Buick with Valve in Head tag, celluloid, Whitehead and Hoag, button–1" diameter, tag–3/4" wide and 1 3/8" high, $75; *(right)* Buick, celluloid, St. Louis Button Co., 7/8" diameter, $35.

Pinback Buttons: *(left)* Cole, lithograph tin, oval, 1 1/8" x 3/4", $65; *(center)* Davis, celluloid, Parisian Novelty Co., 1" diameter, $75; *(right)* Own a Dort, celluloid, Cruver Mfg. Co., 7/8" diameter, $50.

Pinback Buttons:
(left) The New Ford, celluloid, Whitehead and Hoag, 7/8" diameter, $50; *(center)* Ford, celluloid, St. Louis Button Co., 3/4" diameter, $35; *(right)* 1932 Ford, lithograph tin, Geraghty and Co., 3/4" diameter, $35.

Pinback Button, Knox, celluloid, Ehrman Mfg. Co., 1 1/4" diameter, $75.

Pinback Buttons: *(left)* Ford V8 "Aye and Thrifty too!," lithograph tin, 7/8" diameter, $35; *(center)* Methodist Ford Auto Club, celluloid, 3/8" diameter, $100; *(right)* Ford Good Drivers League, lithograph tin, 3/4" diameter, $35.

Pinback Button, Mason Motor Car Company, celluloid, Cruver Mfg. Co., 1 1/2" diameter, $75.

Pinback Button, Harrisburg Automobile Co., celluloid, Weber Badge and Novelty Co., 1 1/4" diameter, $65.

Pinback Button, McFarlan Six, celluloid, 1 1/4" diameter, $75.

Pinback Button, I Want a Maxwell, celluloid, Whitehead and Hoag, 1 1/4" diameter, $50.

Pinback Button, Moon, celluloid, St. Louis Button Co., 1 1/2" diameter, $50–60.

Pinback Button, Montgomery Ward & Co. Electric Horseless Carriage, celluloid, 1 1/4" diameter, $50–60.

Pinback Button, National, celluloid, oval, 1 3/4" x 1 1/4", $60–70.

Pinback Button, Overland, celluloid, Whitehead and Hoag, oval, 1 1/2" x 1 1/4", $50–60.

Pinback Button, Paige, celluloid, attached red, white, and blue celluloid ribbon, Whitehead and Hoag, button-1" diameter, ribbon-1 1/4" wide, 2" long including button, $75.

Pinback Button, You Can Do It with a Reo, celluloid, 1 1/4", $50–60.

Pinback Buttons: (left) Studebaker, wheel motif, celluloid, Bastian Bros., 7/8" diameter, $65; (center) stickpin, Studebaker, brass, Whitehead and Hoag, button–7/8" diameter, 2 1/8" overall height, $75; (right) Studebaker, star motif, celluloid, Bastian Bros., 1" diameter, $65.

Pinback Buttons: *(left)* Champion Studebaker, lithograph tin, L. J. Imber Co., 1" diameter, $35; *(center)* Studebaker, lithograph tin, 7/8" diameter, $25; *(right)* 1938 Studebaker, America's First Low Priced Luxury Car, lithograph tin, Greenduck, 7/8" diameter, $35.

Pinback Buttons: *(top left)* Built Like a Watch, Elgin, brass and enamel, Greenduck, 5/8" diameter, $65; *(top center)* Hudson Super Six, triangle shape, brass and enamel, Whitehead and Hoag, 1/2" tip to tip, $50; *(top right)* Match Packard 120 Against the Field, rectangular shape, brass and enamel, Burr, Pamerson, and Auld Co., 1/2" x 7/8", $100; *(bottom left)* Oakland, brass and enamel, oval, 3/4" x 1/2", $50; *(bottom right)* Reo, shield shape, brass and enamel, Greenduck, 5/8" x 1/2", $60.

Pinback Buttons: *(left)* Lambert, Shore & Beach, celluloid, St. Louis Button Co., 1" diameter, $60; *(center)* Velie Auto, celluloid, Whitehead and Hoag, 1" diameter, $65; *(right)* Roach & Barnes, celluloid, Whitehead and Hoag, 7/8" diameter, $65.

Pinback Buttons: *(left)* Oakland, lithograph tin, 7/8" diameter, $50; *(center)* Whippet, celluloid, 3/4" diameter, $35; *(right)* Rickenbacker, celluloid, Bastian Bros., 7/8" diameter, $65.

Pinback Buttons: *(left)* Marmon, celluloid, Whitehead and Hoag, oval, 1" x 1 1/2", $65; *(center)* Mitchell Six, celluloid, diecut car shape, 1 5/8" x 1/2", $75; *(right)* The MacArthur-Zollars Motor Co., MaxZ, lithograph tin, Whitehead and Hoag, 7/8" diameter, $35.

Pinback Buttons: *(top left)* Durant, brass and enamel, shield shape, Whitehead and Hoag, 3/8" x 5/8", $55; *(top right)* Jewett, brass and enamel, G. A. Miller/Sydney, 5/8" x 3/8", $60; *(bottom left)* Overland, brass and enamel, oval, 7/8" x 5/8", $65; *(bottom right)* The American Four, brass and enamel, shield shape, Boston Regalia Co., 1/2" x 5/8", $75.

Pinback Button, George Vanderbilt Cup Race, celluloid, 1 3/4" diameter, $75.

Pinback Button, Franklin Field Day, 1910, celluloid, Brainbridge Badges and Buttons, 1 3/4" diameter, $75.

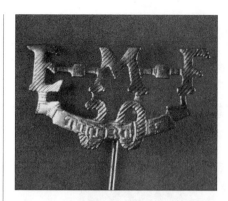

Stickpin, EMF (Everitt, Metzger, Flanders), stamped brass, Grammes, 1" wide, $35.

Stickpin, Glide, stamped brass, Grammes, 2" wide, $35.

Stickpin, Hudson, stamped brass, Grammes, triangular shape, 3/4" tip to tip, $35.

Stickpin, Studebaker, stamped brass, Grammes, 2 1/2" wide, $35.

Stickpins

■

Grammes, located in Allentown, Pennsylvania, was a major manufacturer of metal stamped products, ranging from paper clips to stickpins. About twenty years ago, as Grammes was going out of business, a warehouse find was made of numerous automobile-related stickpins. A sampling ends the illustrations in this chapter.

Stickpin, Cutting, stamped brass, Grammes, 2" wide, $35.

PAPER COLLECTIBLES: AUTOMOTIVE ADVERTISING AND PROMOTIONAL ITEMS

Paper collectibles are one of the hottest collecting segments in the antiques and collectibles field in the mid-1990s. Automobilia paper is one of the reasons. Go to any paper show; you will find the automobile image everywhere—from advertising trade cards to valentines.

Some segments of the paper market have become pricey. Pre-1940 automobile catalogs featuring dozens of plates and photographs, one-sheet advertising posters (European or American), and pre-1940 racing items are a few examples.

However, there is an affordable category for every pricey one. Magazine tear sheets, poster stamps with their vivid graphics, and photographs from family albums usually can be purchased in the $5 to $20 range. Penny dreadful and postcard valentines along with many postcards themselves also fit this price category.

Buy quality. Remember, you are dealing

with printed items; there are few one-of-a-kind anything. Unless extremely scarce, hold out for paper examples in fine or better condition.

Many paper items are purchased for matting and framing. As a result, a premium is charged for larger format items, such as magazine tear sheets from *Country Life* and *Fortune*. Likewise, the graphic quality of the piece also heavily influences price.

But not every piece of paper is collected solely for the image on its surface. Paper also has a reference value. Owners of a particular type of car will attempt to acquire as much research material about their favorite automobile as they can. These buyers create a strong market for repair manuals, sales brochures, and promotional giveaways.

Photographs are one of the hottest areas within paper collectibles. Large size, professional factory photographs, and pre-1940 racing photographs have reached a pricing plateau where $25 to $50 buys the common examples. Family album photographs are where the bargains exist, as well as some of the really great photographs.

Advertising by Company

AUTOMOBILE MANUFACTURERS

Buick, lantern slide, circa 1920s, $35–40. The clear spot in the upper right corner allowed for the insertion of a new number as the cost of the car changed. Buick was part of General Motors at this time.

Brush, window transfer, Brush Runabout, 1911, $175–200. Prior to starting his own company, Alanson Brush was a designer for Oakland. The cost of a Brush single cylinder runabout equaled that of a horse and buggy. The Brush had a wooden frame, wooden axle, and single-coil suspension over each wheel. United States Motor Corporation acquired Brush in 1910.

Chalmers Motor Company (1908–1924), Detroit, Michigan, paperweight, brass, Whitehead and Hoag, circa 1920s, $65–$75. Maxwell acquired Chalmers; Chrysler eventually acquired Maxwell.

Chevrolet,
brochure, Baby
Grand Touring Car,
General Motors,
Flint, Michigan,
$65–75.

Chevrolet, postcard, advertising, 50 Millionth General Motors Car, 1955 Bel Air Sport Coupe, gold, $8–10.

(Left) Chevrolet, *(right)* Chrysler, brochures from 1933 Chicago Century of Progress World's Fair, $15–20 each.

Chevrolet, brochure, Distinguished Beauty, $65–75.

Crosley, brochure, The Car of Tomorrow, $15–20.

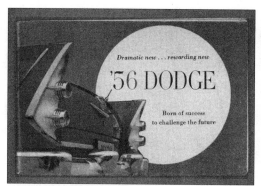

Dodge, catalog, miniature, 1956, soft cover, full color, 32 pages, single page devoted to each model, 5" x 3 1/4", $8–10.

Federal Motor Truck Company, brochure, $20–25.

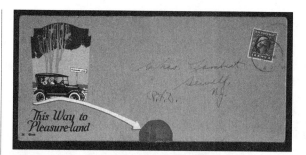

Ford, brochure, The Gateway to the Pleasures of Motors, $40–45.

Ford, bank, Ford Savings Enrollment Plan, reads "Own a Ford/The First Step/Bank a coin a day./Ford Easy Purchase Plan," circa 1920s, $125–150.

Ford, brochure, Model A, 1930, $50–60.

Ford, catalog, 1913, $75. By 1913 Ford was producing 1,000 cars a day. The catalog contains the following: "Notice—owing to our inability to secure a satisfactory speedometer, our cars will not be equipped with them for the present. An allowance of $6.00 will be made to the purchaser on Ford cars not equipped with speedometer. Signed Ford Motor Co."

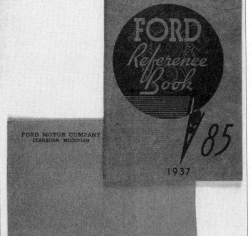

Ford, 1937 Ford Reference Book, slip case, $35–40.

Ford, construction set, F. S. Rode Company, Jeannette, Pennsylvania, Build a Ford Toy, $175–200. Tin disk, race course for marble, and wooden pegs, put peg in location where marble stops, thus eventually building a car from the parts designated.

Ford, cup, plastic, two layers with full-color printed paper insert, West Bend Thermo Serv, Inc., 1968/69, Ford logo, dated 1968, 2 3/4" top diameter, 6 3/8" high, $10. The most recent car pictured is the 1969 LTD four-door hardtop.

Ford, dealer's business card, circa 1920s, 3 1/4" x 2 1/4", $10–15.

Ford, Model T chocolate candy mold, Shemyer Company, circa 1915, $125–150.

Ford dealer, table lamp, rotates as a result of heat generated by light bulb, three different advertisements, Buy A Ford, And See The Difference, Better Days Are Coming—Also Weather, $350–400.

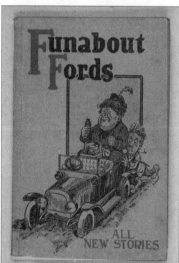

Ford, books, *(above, left) Funny Stories About the Ford: Uncanny Stories About a Canny Car,* Presto Publishing Co., Volume II, 1915, $20–25, publisher states, "Each of the humorists and cartoonists agree that the Ford is a rattling good car"; *(above, right) More Funabout Fords: A Ford is something like a wealthy baby. It has a new rattle every day,* Howell Company, Chicago, Illinois, 1915, $20–25; *(left) Funabout Fords: All New Stories—It is impossible to get arrested in the city for speeding in a Ford, but be careful about rushing the car,* Albert Whiteman and Company, Chicago, Illinois, 1921, $20–25.

Ford, bronze, *(left)* Ford's 50th Anniversary, 1903–1953, $50; *(right)* Henry Ford, $50.

Ford, magazine, *Ford Times,* centennial issue, July 1963, soft cover, full color, 64 pages, 5" x 7", $15.

Ford, sheet music, "The Little Ford Rambled Right Along," words by C. R. Foster and Byron Gay, music by Byron Gay, C. R. Foster Publishing, Los Angeles, California, circa 1915, $20–25.

Ford, postcards, comic, Commercial Colortype Company, Cobb Shinn illustrator, poke fun at the Model "T," circa 1915, $7 each. *(Upper left)* A Ford is like a bathtub, you don't like to be seen in one; *(upper right)* Even the birds know a Ford when they see one —cheap, cheap; *(lower left)* You needn't cover it up, Mister, I saw what kind it was; *(lower right)* A Future President.

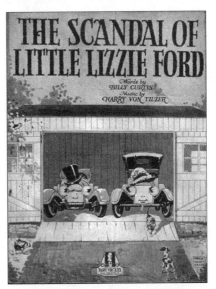

Ford, sheet music, "The Scandal of Little Lizzie Ford," words by Billy Curtis, music by Harry Von Tilzer, Von Tilzer Publishing Co., 1921, $20–25.

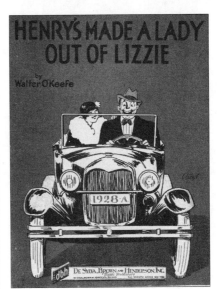

Ford, sheet music, "Henry's Made a Lady Out of Lizzie," by Walter O'Keefe DeSylva, published by Brown & Henderson, Inc., New York, introducing the Model A Ford of 1928, $20–$25

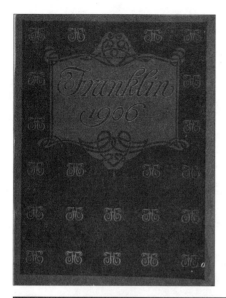

Franklin (1902–1934), H. H. Franklin Manufacturing Company, Syracuse, New York, brochure, 1906, $275–300.

Franklin, brochure, Supercharged Airman Series, $65–75.

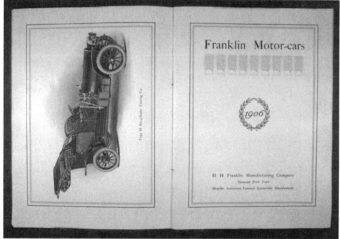

Franklin, pocket knife, The Franklin Car/Mack Truck, made for local dealer in Lancaster, Pennsylvania, $45–50.

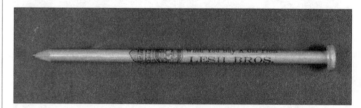

Graham Paige, novelty, pencil, U Hit the Nail on the Head When You Buy a Car from Lesh Brothers Motors, $15–20. The Graham brothers acquired Paige in 1927. In 1934 Graham Paige offered a super-charged Graham Paige with a top speed of 95 mph.

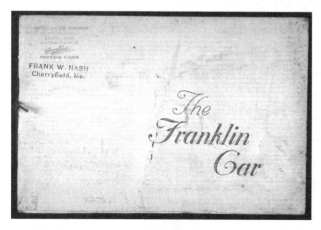

Franklin, brochure, 1918, $100–$125. The Franklin was air-cooled and often referred to as a doctor's car.

King, glass slide, circa 1920s, $35–40. King was a pioneer automobile designer. After serving as superintendent of the Northern Motor Car Company, he organized the King Auto Company in 1910.

Lexington, glass slide, Minute Man Six, circa 1920, $35–40. The slide bears the notation "Connersville, Indiana."

Lexington, glass slide, circa 1920s, $35–40. The Auburn Company acquired Lexington in 1928.

Maxwell Motor Company (1904–1925), Detroit, Michigan, children's book, *The Maxwell Book for Kiddies,* 1917 publication date, $50–60.

Maxwell Motor Company, catalog and repair manual, 1916 *Catalogue and Service Book,* $40–45. Benjamin Briscoe combined 130 separate companies, including Maxwell, into his United States Motor Car Corporation in 1910. Walter P. Chrysler acquired the Maxwell portion of U.S. Motor Car Corp. in 1921. The Maxwell became the Chrysler 4 in 1926 and the Plymouth in 1929.

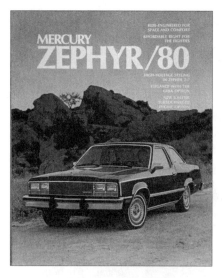

Mercury, brochure, 1980 Zephyr, soft cover, full color, 11 pages, 8 1/2" x 11", $5.

Packard, brochure, 1907, The Flight of "Thirty" (30 hp Packard), chronicles a road race from Detroit to Chicago and back, total time of 20 hours and 35 minutes, car driven by Montague Roberts, winning driver of the 1908 Around the World Race, $75.

Nash (1917–1957), record, front and back, Nash advertising promotion for Straight-8 with coil ignition and overhead valves, 1932, $60–70.

Packard, catalog, Twin-Six, $65–75.

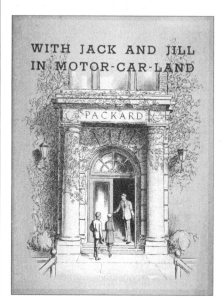

Packard, children's book, *Child's Book on the History of Packard: Ask the Man Who Owns One*, circa 1933, $65–75.

Packard, promotional mechanical advertising card, Luxurious Motoring, as you open it the card car moves forward, $175–200.

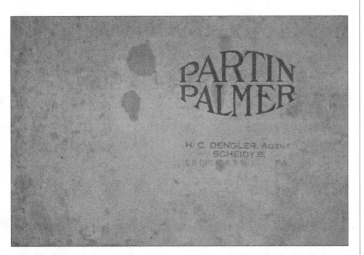

Partin Palmer, made by Commonwealth Motor Company, Rochelle, Illinois, catalog, circa 1917, $65–75.

Pierce Arrow, George N. Pierce Company, Buffalo, New York, catalog, 1905 Great Arrow, $225–250.

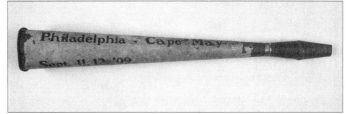

Premier Automobile Company, advertising horn, given for race run on September 11 and 12, 1909, between Philadelphia and Cape May, New Jersey, $65–75.

Rambler, made by Thomas B. Jeffery and Co., Kenosha, Wisconsin, 1907 sales catalog, $125–150.

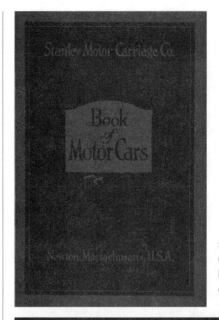

Rambler, *Rambler* magazine, 1908, distributed to Rambler owners, $100–125.

Stanley Motor Carriage Company, Newton, Massachusetts, sales catalog, *Book of Motor Cars,* $90–100.

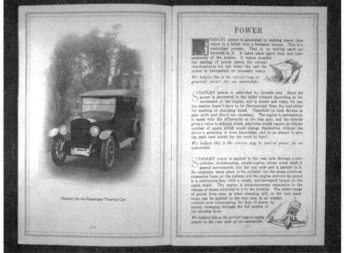

Stanley Motor Carriage Company, booklet, *1923 Questions and Answers,* $75.

Star and Durant, both made by Durant Motor Company, *(left)* Star, catalog, $50; *(center)* Durant, catalog, $50; *(right)* price guide folder for Durant and Star cars, $30.

Studebaker, promotional mechanical advertising card, Studebaker Duplex model, automobile converts from sedan to open car, $75.

Studebaker, South Bend, Indiana, 1923 catalog, $75–85. Studebaker made its first gas-powered automobile in 1904. Previously they manufactured electric cars beginning in 1902. Studebaker's 1902 electric car was two passenger, chain driven, and tiller steered.

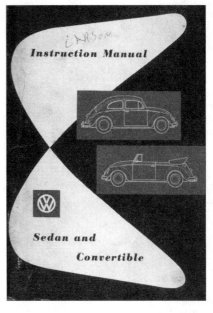

Volkswagen, instruction manual for sedan and convertible, 1960, soft cover, black and white with blue insert, 88 pages, 5 5/8" x 7 7/8", $12–15.

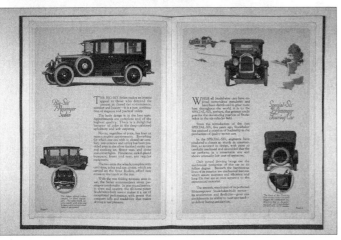

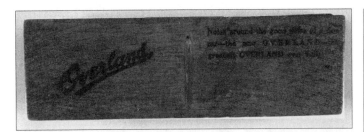

Willys-Knight (1914–1932), Toledo, Ohio, clapper (noisemaker), obverse and reverse, demonstrates how noisy other cars are when compared to the noiseless Willys-Knight double sleeve-valve engine, "The engine is smooth and silent as the shadows of night," $65–75.

TIRE MANUFACTURERS

Firestone, brochure, 1939/40 New York World's Fair, 1939, $15.

Goodrich, Silverstone, tire ashtray, $45–50.

Goodrich, prints, series of four, each print features the Goodrich brothers, circa 1902, $175–200 per print.

Untitled, parked car, two Goodrich Brothers sitting beside road, one playing violin and other playing a guitar, sign on wall that says "Pan-American Exposition," 21 1/2" x 14 1/2".

Untitled, Goodrich Brothers driving car with four passengers, 26 1/2" x 17 1/2".

Untitled, Goodrich Brothers in a boat fishing, 24" x 16 1/2".

"The Goodrich Rubber Man's Vacation," Goodrich officials in balloon, elephant being lifted by balloon, 19" x 26".

Good Year, brochure, *How to Select an Automobile Tire*, circa 1910, $10–15.

United States Tire, tire ashtray, nickel-plated rim and tread, $50–75.

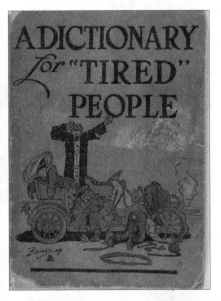

Good Year, *A Dictionary for "Tired" People*, illustrated by Briggs, an artist whose work also appears on comic automobile postcards, circa 1910, $30.

Advertising by Type

Blotters, *(top)* Whippet, a product of the Willys-Overland Company, Toledo, Ohio; *(bottom)* Rush Motor Truck Company; both circa 1925, $15–20 each.

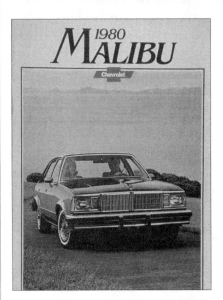

Brochure, Chevrolet, 1980 Malibu, soft cover, full color, 15 pages, 8 1/2" x 11", $5.

Kelly Springfield, booklet, *The Kant Slip Motor Goose*, $60.

Brochures, manufacturers of automobile electrical parts, *(upper left)* Delco, Garage Electrical Plant, *(lower left)* Eisemann, Magneto, *(center)* Gray and Davis, Electrical Systems, *(upper right)* Bosch, Magneto, *(lower right)* K. W. Ignition, 1912, $10–15 each.

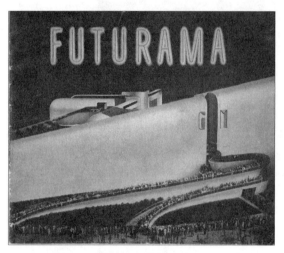

Brochure, General Motors, GM pavilion, 1939/40 New York World's Fair, $15–20.

Brochure, International Body Works, Chicago, Illinois, custom bodies for Ford and Chevrolet chassis, circa 1925, $25.

Brochures, *(left)* Fireman's Fund Insurance, *4 Wheel Fun,* 1929, $20; *(center)* Gulf, *Record of Lubrication,* 1920s, $15; *(right)* Franklin, advertisement for spare tires, $30.

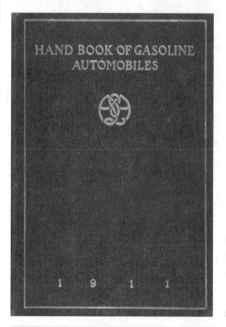

Catalog, Automobile Manufacturers' Association, licensee, *1911 Hand Book of Gasoline Automobiles,* $100.

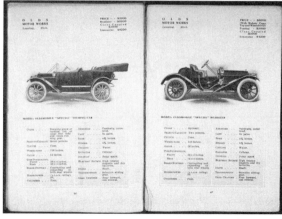

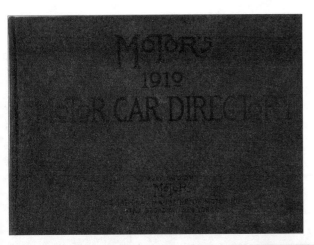

Fan, lady drives roadster from which a banner is advertising *Excuse My Dust,* a movie playing at the Cozy Theatre, $60–70.

Catalog, *The National Magazine of Motoring, Motor's 1910 Motor Car Directory*, $90–100.

Catalog Plates, *Coach Builders, Wheelwrights and Motor Car Mfg. Auto Journal*, 1898, company made custom bodies, $60–70 each.

Fan, flapper (siren) seated in 1920s car, advertisement on fan for Marrell Inns, $25–30.

Fobs, watch, *(left)* Fordson Tractor, $50; *(right)* American Champion Thomas Flyer, the car that won the 1908 New York to Paris race, $150–175.

Magazine Tear Sheets remain one of the most affordable automobile collectibles. They can be used to trace the development of the automobile from its early days to the present. You have a hundred years of material from which to choose. Nineteen ninety-six marks the centennial year of the manufacturing of automobiles in the United States.

Magazine Tear Sheet, Cadillac, convertible with red body and white interior, black four-door sedan, *Fortune,* June 1963, 10 1/4" x 12 7/8", $4.

Magazine Tear Sheet, Packard, *Ladies Home Journal,* early 1930s, $5–10. As the story goes, Packard purchased an 1898 Winton. He was not pleased with the performance so he wrote to the Winton Company only to receive a reply, "If you can build a better one, you should." He did. His first car is on display at Lehigh University in Bethlehem, Pennsylvania. It still runs. Packards were made between 1899 and 1958.

Magazine Tear Sheet, Edsel, 1960 Ford Edsel for 1960, $5–10. The Edsel was introduced by Ford's Lincoln Mercury division for the 1958 buying season. In spite of the vast sums spent on customer research and public relations, the Edsel failed. Production of the Edsel ceased shortly after the announcement of the 1960 models.

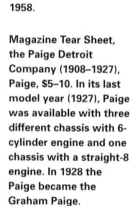

Magazine Tear Sheet, the Paige Detroit Company (1908–1927), Paige, $5–10. In its last model year (1927), Paige was available with three different chassis with 6-cylinder engine and one chassis with a straight-8 engine. In 1928 the Paige became the Graham Paige.

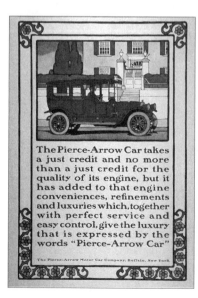

Magazine Tear Sheet, Pierce Arrow, *Country Life,* 1913, $10–15. *Country Life* contains some of the best early automobile advertisements. Pierce manufactured automobiles from 1901 to 1938. Prior to 1909 when Pierce Arrow was first used, the car was known initially as the Pierce Motorette and then the Pierce Great Arrow. It was America's prestige car for many years.

Magazine Tear Sheet, Plymouth, Belvedere Sports Sedan, four-door hardtop, *Holiday,* March 1956, 10 3/4" x 13 5/8", $4. Furs by Maximilian.

Magazine Tear Sheet, Stutz, *Country Life,* circa 1920s, $10–15. The Ideal Motor Car Company made the first Stutz racing cars. The company changed its name to Stutz Motor Car in 1913.

Magazine Tear Sheet, Plymouth Horizon TC, red body, two-page spread, *Sports Illustrated,* February 12, 1979, 16 1/4" x 10 7/8", $2–3. This was the first American sport coupe with front-wheel drive.

Magazine Tear Sheet, Rambler, *Country Life,* circa 1905, $5–10. Thomas B. Jeffery and Co., Kenosha, Wisconsin, made the Rambler. Nash acquired Rambler and was itself eventually acquired by American Motors.

Maps, *(left to right):* Esso, Pennsylvania, Cathedral of Learning, University of Pittsburgh, full-color cover image, 24 panels, folded measures 3 7/8" x 8 1/4", 1946, $5–8; Esso, Delaware/Maryland/Virginia/WestVirginia, Baltimore's Fort McHenry, full-color cover image, 24 panels, folded measures 4 1/8" x 8 1/2", 1948, $5–8; Sunoco, Pennsylvania, generic cover, full-color cover image, 24 panels, folded measures 3 7/8" x 8 1/8", 1946, $5–8. The first appearance of an interstate highway on a road map was in 1952. Collectors are focusing largely on maps from the 1930s through the early 1950s. Collectors only want mint examples. Any damage immediately makes a map landfill material.

Mirrors, advertising, *(upper left)* Everitt Metzger Flanders Company, Detroit, Michigan,. marketed by Studebaker, circa 1910, $50; *(upper right)* American Motor Car Company, American Underslung, "No noise but the wind," Harry C. Stutz, who later founded the Stutz Motor Company, designed the American Underslung, $90–100; *(center)* Mack Truck, circa 1910, $75; *(lower left)* Rutenberg Motor Company, Marion, Indiana, pictures race car motor designed by Russell Rutenberg, the Glide was one of several cars using engines designed by Rutenberg, 1903, $50; *(lower right)* Paterson (1908–1923), Flint, Michigan, "30"-horsepower, 4-cylinder car with sliding gear transmission and shaft drive, Paterson developed the 30-hp, 4-cylinder engine by 1910, $50.

Novelties, *(left)* notepad, Columbus Buggy Company (1903–1913), Columbus, Ohio, $35–40; *(right)* pack of soap sheets, promotional giveaway from Wink Motor Car Company, Allentown, Pennsylvania, a dealer for Cole, Buick and Nash, $15–20.

Novelties, *(top)* pen, advertising the Carter Car, "The Car Ahead," $35–40; *(center)* ruler, folding, celluloid, advertising Glide, made between 1903 and 1920, used a 40-horsepower, 6-cylinder Rutenberg engine between 1915 and 1920, $35–40; *(bottom)* whistle, Flint Auto, made by Durant between 1923 and 1927, $35–40.

Nothing captures the importance of the automobile more than the large volume of photographs in which it appeared. The family's first car, a trip to the country, any unusual happening—all were captured on film.

Value increases when a specific car and model can be identified. While some collectors limit their purchases to professionally taken photographs, others delight in assembling large collections of family snapshots.

Photograph, Chrysler, insurance company photograph, early Chrysler after an accident, 10" x 8", 1936, $40–45.

Photograph, Ford, 8" x 6", mounted on card, circa 1908, $65–75.

Photograph, Ford, country showroom; also includes tractor and washing machines, 9 1/2" x 6 1/2", mounted on card, circa 1923, $65–75.

Photograph, Ford, service garage, 8" x 6", mounted on card, circa 1912, $65–75.

Photograph, Ford, Bell Telephone Model "T" service truck, 7" x 5", mounted on trimmed card, circa 1913, $65–75.

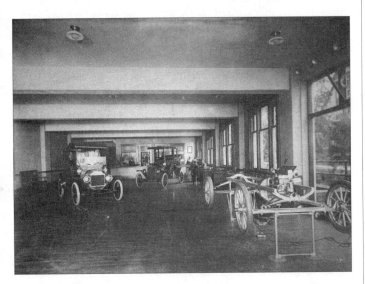

Photograph, Ford, city showroom and service garage, 8" x 6", mounted on card, circa 1912, $100.

Photograph, Great Western, 1911 Great Western in ditch, $100.

Photograph, Grout, gasoline car, company also made steam cars, 9 3/8" x 7 3/4", mounted on card, circa 1910, $75.

Photograph, Mercury, postcard, 1977 Cougar Brougham, four-door pillared hardtop, $8–10. By the late 1950s the full-color, glossy, photographic-image posters, prints, and postcards replaced the pre-war black-and-white manufacturers' promotional photographs.

Photograph, Haynes Apperson Surrey, 2 cylinder, opposed engine, purchased by Boston manufacturer at the first New York auto show in 1900, 7" x 5", mounted on card, $90–100.

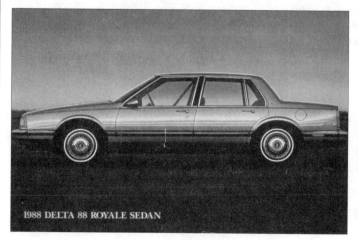

Photograph, Oldsmobile, postcard, 1988 Delta 88 Royale Sedan, $8–10. Photographic-image postcards are an inexpensive form of advertising. Most are found with a dealer's imprint on the back. Interestingly, most were never mailed, but were used instead as showroom giveaways.

Photograph, Hudson, sales promotion photograph; speedster custom body, 9 1/2" x 8", circa 1927, $45–50.

Photograph, Packard, 16 1/2" x 9 1/2", mounted on card, $75. Notice dual windshield.

Photograph, Peerless, factory interior, 4 3/4" x 3 3/4", mounted on card, circa 1905, $45–50.

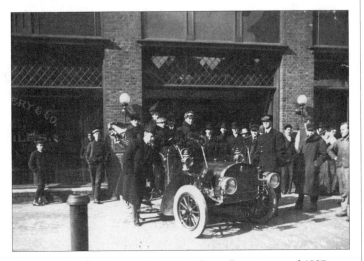

Photograph, Rambler outside Jeffery Show Room, start of 1907 Glidden Tour, 8 1/2" x 6 1/2", $50.

Photograph, Stanley Steamer, factory photograph, 10" x 8", 1920s, $50–60.

Photograph, Stearns, 50-horsepower car at end of Glidden Tour, 10" x 7 3/4", $40–50. Charles J. Glidden, a telephone entrepreneur who helped develop the Bell system, was an avid car enthusiast. He established several endurance runs, known as Glidden Tours. These tours were endurance, not speed tests, designed to publicize the need for good roads.

Photograph, Stevens Duryea, receiving delivery of 1913 Stevens Duryea from railroad boxcar, Mauch Chunk, Pennsylvania, 14" x 11", mounted on card, $100.

Photograph, generic, 10" x 8", mounted on card, approximately 1898, $75–100.

Photograph, generic, country repair shop, 7" x 5", mounted on card, circa late 1920s, $25–30.

Photograph, generic, family in automobile, circa 1905, $30–50.

Photograph, generic, staged commercial picture, William Johnson photograph, Atlantic City, numbered #27 on front wheel to identify people in car, 8 1/4" x 6", mounted on card, $25–35.

Photograph, generic, early limousine being pulled out of mud, from family photograph album, 4 1/4" x 3 3/4", circa 1910, $15–20.

Photograph, generic, used car lot, 8 3/8" x 4 1/2", circa late 1920s, $25–30.

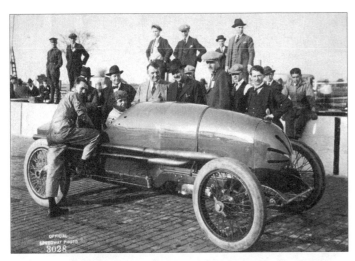

Photograph, Indianapolis Speedway, Peugeot, unidentified driver, 10" x 8", 1921, $35–40.

Photograph, Indianapolis Speedway, Joe Thomas driver, 10" x 8", $35–40.

Photograph, Indianapolis Speedway, Howard Wilcox, 10" x 8", circa 1921, $35–40.

Photograph, racers on dirt track, Wilmington, Delaware, 9 1/2" x 5 1/2", mounted on card, 1916, $45–50.

Postcards are a wonderful automobilia specialty. However, the category is extremely large. Specialize from the beginning.

Advertising (factory), art, and comic postcards are just a few of the categories worth considering. While the most obvious approach is to collect postcards by automobile manufacturer, this is one of the more expensive categories, especially for early material.

Many automobiles came in series. Completing a small series and having it matted and framed makes an excellent conversation piece.

Real photo postcards, i.e., postcards that are really photographic prints on postcard stock, are currently very much in vogue. Premium prices are paid for real photo postcards featuring clear, distinct images of pre–World War I cars.

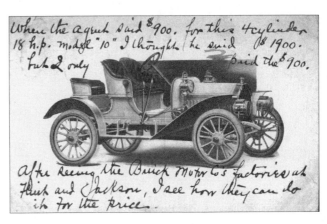

Postcard, advertising, Buick Motor Company, circa 1908, $35–40.

Postcard, advertising, Ford, Model "T," $20–25.

Postcard, advertising, Hupmobile World Touring Car, $45–50.

Postcard, advertising, Ford, Model "T" at fair, $20–25.

Postcard, advertising, Mack Truck, $50–60.

Postcard, advertising, Hupp Motor Car Company, Hupmobile Coupe, $45–50.

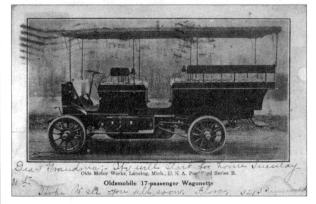

Postcard, advertising, Oldsmobile Wagonette, circa 1910, $35–40.

Postcard, advertising, Plymouth, Barney Oldfield, $15–20.

Postcard, advertising, Warren Detroit, "30"-horsepower model, $35–40.

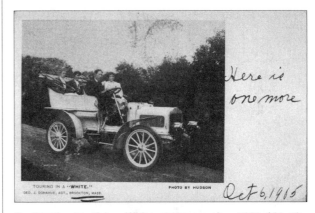

Postcard, advertising, White, steam car, circa 1905, $35–40.

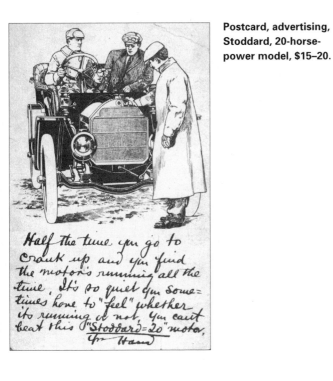

Postcard, advertising, Stoddard, 20-horse-power model, $15–20.

Postcard, advertising, Auto Adjustable Fender, cow catcher for people, $20–25.

Postcard, advertising, Truffault Hartford Shock Absorbers, circa 1910, $20–25.

Postcard, advertising, Truffault Hartford Shock Absorbers, circa 1910, $20–25.

Harry Eliott was a commercial artist, best known for his hunting and early tavern scenes. When motoring became popular during the first decades of the 20th century, Eliott started to paint auto race scenes. Many examples of his work appeared as postcards and prints. The same holds true for the automobile artwork of Lance Thackeray and Stuart Travis, famed *Punch* illustrators.

Postcard, art, Harry Eliott illustrator, $15–20.

Postcard, art, Harry Eliott illustrator, $15–20.

Postcard, art, Harry Eliott illustrator, $15–20.

Postcard, art, Harry Eliott illustrator, $15–20.

Postcard, art, E. Montaut illustrator, $35–40. Montaut, a young artist in Paris, noticed large crowds attending motoring events. As a result, he directed his efforts toward producing automobile and automobile racing art, publishing his prints under the name of Montaut and Atelier. His most famous prints, measuring 17" x 34", were hand colored. It was a logical progression for his art to be featured on postcards of the era. His automobile images date between 1897 and 1913.

Postcard, racing, Paris, Levassor Monument, commemorates first automobile race in France, 1895 Paris to Bordeaux, $25.

Postcard, racing, generic, fairground's race, $25–30.

Postcard, racing, Fairmount Park Race, Philadelphia, Pennsylvania, $15–20.

Postcard, racing, Indianapolis Speedway, Chet Miller, May 26, 1952, Novi Pure Oil Special, qualifying record of 139.034 miles per hour, full color, $8–10.

Postcard, racing, 1908 New York to Paris Race, Times Square, race began on February 12, $30.

Postcard, racing, 1908 New York to Paris Race, Protos, one of two German entries, in Times Square, $30.

Postcard, racing, 1908 New York to Paris Race, Thomas Flyer, the American entry, in Times Square, $30.

Postcard, racing, 1908 New York to Paris Race, Zust, the Italian entry, in Times Square, $30.

Postcard, racing, 1908 New York to Paris Race, Thomas Flyer, Moto Bloc, another of the French entries, and Zust, in New York at start of race, $35.

Postcard, racing, 1908 New York to Paris Race, De Dion, one of the French entries, in Times Square, $30.

Mascot, British Bobby, signed J. Hassall, brass, moveable head and hat to create different expressions, circa 1911, $150–200.

Mascot, Packard type, chrome-plated zinc casting, circa 1948–1951, $15–25.

Ornament, Noma #1500 Christmas Wreath, Noma Electric Corporation, New York, 6" diameter, 6-volt, silk roping, plug into car's cigarette lighter, $75–100.

Vases, pair, silver, English, embossed automobile motif, circa 1908, $450–500 for the pair.

Ashtray, German, 4 1/4" diameter, circa 1905, $75–100.

Hot Chocolate Pot, A. Grouard, Paris, France, children at play motif, auto pictured on one of the pots, 5" x 13 1/2", circa 1905, $1,500–2,000.

Cream and Sugar Set, Beach Boys, marked "applause/MADE IN KOREA/27610/WHEELES/SUGAR & CREAMER," car has yellow body and Chevrolet marking on radiator, trailer with light blue body, yellow surfboard, approx. 8 1/2" long, $15–20.

Stein, German, obverse shows car having just run over some ducks, reverse shows driver negotiating a payment for killed geese, marked "Munchen," $650–750.

Vase, French, frog driver, snails as the power wheels, lily pads as the body, circa 1905, $650–750.

Ashtray, Ford, 1964/65, four models surround shield; *(left to right)* Sports Coupe (tan), Mustang (blue), Torino (red), Four-Door Sedan (blue), 8 1/8" square, dealer's showroom item, $50–60.

Coasters, Ford, 1964/65; *(left)* Sedan, blue body, 3 3/4" diameter, dealer's showroom item, not sold to public, $10, and *(right)* Sports Coupe, tan body, 3 3/4" diameter, dealer's showroom item, not sold to public, $10.

Glass, water, German, hand painted, car running over duck, $75–100.

Perfume Caddy, French, four bottles with gold trim, base with velvet covering, 2 1/2" wide, 1 5/8" high, circa 1905, $225–250.

Soda Pop Can, Coca-Cola, pictures Mario Andretti, 1994, $2.

Watch, pocket, Holly Freres (Switzerland) made case, Elgin (American) works, silver case, relief of touring car traveling on a country road, 2" diameter, circa 1905, $275–300.

Clock, American, Ansonia Clock Company, cast brass, 7 1/2" wide, 5 1/2" high, circa 1905, $350–400.

Clock, Swiss works, tortoise shell face, sterling silver case inlaid with a sterling silver automobile with driver and passenger traveling down a country road, 4 3/8" wide, 3 1/2" high, circa 1906, $275–300.

Driving Club Badge, Corsica, white metal and enamel, six town crests (Bastai, Calvi, Ile Rousse, Sartene, Ajaccio, Corte), 3 1/8" diameter, $35.

Pocket Knife, German, marked "D. Peres / Solingen, Germany," sedan, 2 1/4" long, $45–50.

Driving Club Badge, Royal Automobile Club of Spain, brass, white metal, and enamel, 3" wide, 4" high, $65.

Driving Club Badge, Automobile Club Firenze, brass and enamel, 3 1/2" wide, 3 3/4" high, $75.

Employee Badge, Yellow Cab, shield shape, 2 3/8" x 2 1/2", plated brass, cab with yellow enamel body, black enamel fenders, $50–60.

Pinback Buttons: *(left)* Pontiac—For Economy and Riding Comfort, lithograph tin, 7/8" diameter, $35; *(center top)* It's Spring—Get a Pontiac, lithograph tin, Greenduck, 7/8" diameter, $35; *(center bottom)* New Pontiac—Chief of Values, lithograph tin, 3/4" diameter, $25; *(right)* Pontiac, picture of Indian, celluloid, 7/8" diameter, $25.

Stickpin, Maxwell, stamped brass, Grammes, 2" wide, $35.

Pinback Buttons: *(left)* Chevrolet, winged wheel border motif, celluloid, 3/4" diameter, $35; *(center top)* New Chevrolet Six, lithograph tin, full color, Geraghty and Co., 3/4" diameter, $35; *(center bottom)* Try it, Chevrolet, lithograph tin, 7/8" diameter, $35; *(right)* 1934 Chevrolet, lithograph tin, 7/8" diameter, $35.

Chevrolet, brochure, Distinguished Beauty, $65–75.

Oldsmobile, record, "Sounds of the Tornado," advertising promotion, circa 1970s, $45–50.

Fisk, tire manufacturer, poster, $200–250.

Fan, butterfly with lady driver in center, advertisement on fan for Wrigley's Chewing gum, circa 1900, $45–50.

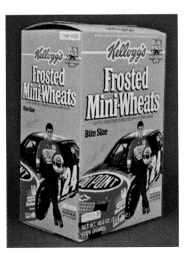

Cereal Box, Kellogg's Frosted Mini-Wheats, 1994, two boxes within outer package, Jeff Gordon, 1993 Winston Cup Rookie of the Year, Dupont No. 24, 7 3/4" x 11 3/4", $8–10.

Magazine Tear Sheet, Studebaker, 1951, $5–10. Studebaker automobiles were made in the United States between 1902 and 1964. Henry and Clem Studebaker, who operated a blacksmith shop in South Bend, Indiana, in the late 19th century, founded the company. Their first cars were electric. They made their first gasoline automobile in 1904. In 1964, production was transferred to Canada. The company closed its door in 1966.

Postcard, advertising, Truffault Hartford Shock Absorbers, circa 1910, $20–25.

Poster, Laurin & Klement, 8" x 10", $10.

Postcard, comic, four-card series, 10 horsepower, $25.

Postcard, comic, four-card series, 20 horsepower, $25.

Sheet Music, Buick, "Take Me on a Buick Honeymoon" by Art Hickman, words by Ben Black, published by the Howard Automobile Company, 1922, $50. The Howard Automobile Company was a distributor of Buick cars in San Francisco, Portland, Oakland, and Los Angeles, California.

Postcard, comic, four-card series, 40 horsepower, $25.

Postcard, comic, four-card series, 60 horsepower, $25.

Cast-iron Toy, Arcade, Andy Gump #348, enameled with a bright snappy red body with green trim, white wheels with green center, red hubs, circa 1920s, $2,250–2,500. Originally sold for $0.89. The *Chicago Tribune* syndicated "The Gumps."

Die Cast Hot Wheels, Mattel, Computer Cars, Rigor-Motor, initial series of six cars ('93 Camaro, Power Pistons, Hydroplane, '96 Mustang, and Oscar Mayer Wienermobile), period blister pack measuring 6" x 10", 1996, $5.

Die Cast Tootsie Toy, custom-built Hi-Way Henry utilizing a Tootsie Toy chassis, mid-1980s, $125–150. Less than ten of these reconstructed toys were made.

Clockwork Toy, lithograph tin, Fischer, German, trademarked "Nifty," Hi-Way Henry, 10 1/2" long, circa late 1920s, $3,500–4,000. A toy distributor contracted with Fischer to produce this comic strip character toy. It sold new for $1. Reproduction Alert: This toy was reproduced in 1995.

Clockwork Toy, Japanese, marked "Japan KKK Cragstan," roadster, blue body, battery-powered electric headlights and motor, box marked "Golden Beam," $150–175.

Clockwork Toy, painted tin, French, clockwork motor makes the driver wave her arms, driver has bisque head, 8 3/4" long, circa 1895, $3,000–3,500.

Clockwork Toy, lithograph tin, German, Buffalo Bill driving an automobile, 9 1/2" long, circa 1898, $4,500–5,000. Pictured in Histoire de L'Automobilisme, a book published in France in 1898. Buffalo Bill included an automobile as part of his famed Wild West Show during a tour of France in the late 1890s.

Penny Toy, lithograph tin, German, limousine, blue body with yellow trim, chauffeur and passengers, 4 1/2" wide, 2 3/8" high, circa 1905, $125–150.

Pull Toy, lithograph tin, H. D. Beach, Coshocton, Ohio, Moxie Horsemobile, red body, wheels on tabs (when in up position, car is stationary; when down, wheels turn), 8" wide, 6 1/2" high, circa 1920s, $250–300. The toy came in a carton with an advertisement touting "Drink Moxie for your health." The toy also comes in blue.

Game car, Milton Bradley, Peter Coddle's Trip, select slips of paper to fill in text blanks from story booklet, circa 1923, $65–75.

Game, card, Parker Brothers, Touring, 3rd Edition, circa 1927, $45–55. This card game is extremely common.

Postcard, racing, 1908 New York to Paris Race, winner Thomas Flyer, $30.

Postcard, advertising/racing, Thomas Flyer, winner of 1908 New York to Paris Race, $45.

Postcard, racing, Ormond Beach, Florida, $25–30.

Postcard, racing, 1907 Peking to Paris Race, won by the 24-horsepower Itala, an Italian car driven by Prince Borghese, $35.

Postcard, racing, generic, auto polo, $35–40.

Large advertising posters are expensive and difficult to find, especially those dating before 1940. Because of their scarcity, they are not included in this volume.

However, 1920s issues of *Motor,* an automobile magazine published in both the United States and Europe, included miniature advertising posters, usually measuring 9 1/2" x 12 3/4", as part of its regular fare. These miniature advertising posters are very colorful and affordable. Here is a sampling.

Poster, Auto Federn Steirische Gusstahlwerk, $10.

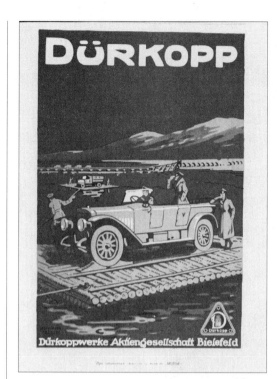

Poster, Dürkopp, $10.

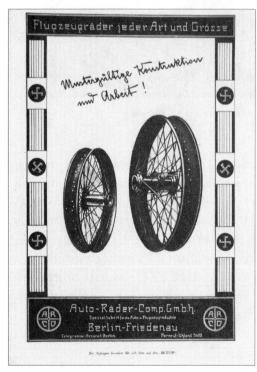

Poster, Auto Räder Comp., $10.

Poster, Lanz Tractors, $10.

Poster, Schebera, $10.

In 1908 *Motor* featured a series of prints of French lithographs picturing automobile scenes. The series lasted for one year.

Print, 1908 *Motor*, Elopement, 13 3/4" x 9 1/4", $45–50.

Premium Stamps, Top Value Stamp Booklet, 5 1/2" x 6 1/2", full color (front and back) spread, late 1960s, $5 for book filled with stamps. Many service stations offered premium stamps as a way of encouraging repeat business. There were several national and numerous local varieties. The artwork on many booklets featured the principal stamp outlets—the supermarket, drug store, and gas station.

Print, 1908 *Motor*, La Vache Curieuse, 9 1/4" x 13 3/4", $45–50.

Print, 1908 *Motor*, Un Match Inattendor, copyright 1907, 13 3/4" x 9 1/4", $45–50.

Print, 1908 *Motor*, Le Dejever, E. Montaut illustrator, 13 3/4" x 9 1/4", $45–50.

Print, 1908 *Motor*, Une Romorque, 13 3/4" x 9 1/4", $45–50.

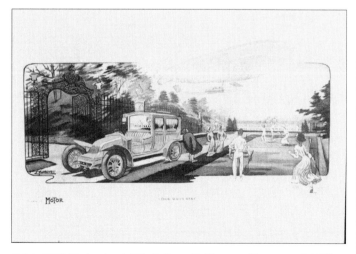

Print, 1908 *Motor*, Look Who's Here, E. Montaut illustrator, 9 1/4" x 13 3/4", $45–50.

Print, 1908 *Motor*, Wheel & Wheel, 13 3/4" x 9 1/4", $45–50.

Print, 1908 Motor, untitled, Thor illustrator, 9 1/4" x 13 3/4", $45–50.

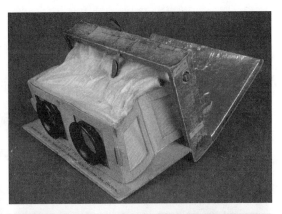

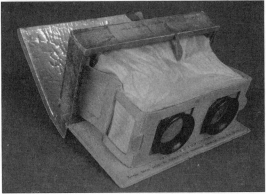

Salesman's Factory Stereoview Kit showing the French 1907 De Dion. Collapses into leather-covered box for transportability, when opened serves as a viewer for stereoview series showing manufacturing steps of De Dion automobiles, $750.

The thrill and romance of the automobile were quickly picked up by Tin Pan Alley. Music appeared in every imaginable tempo. There were comic songs, waltzes, two-steps, rags, romantic songs, etc. While there is no master list of sheet music for songs about the automobile, with an automobile term in the title, or with automobile graphics on the cover, the number must be in the middle to high hundreds.

Most sheet music covers had great graphics. It is the graphic, more than anything else, that give value to this material.

Automobile manufacturers sponsored many of these songs as a means to promote their product. The songwriters did not hesitate to point out that if you owned a certain model car, you would do quite well with the ladies, e.g., the 1927 "Get 'Em in a Rumble Seat," with lyrics by Jack Marshall.

Do not overlook period cylinder records or 78 rpm records featuring these original songs. Locating pre-1915 records featuring automobile songs requires patience and diligence. In all my years of collecting I have only five in my collection.

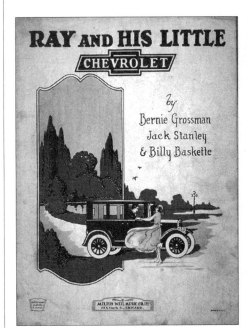

Sheet Music, Chevrolet, "Ray and His Little Chevrolet" by Bernie Grossman, Jack Stanley, and Billy Baskette, Milton Weil Music Company publishers, also available on piano rolls and records, 1924, $50. Ray bought a little coupe for chickens and he always gets the choicest pickins.

Sheet Music, Chevrolet, "See the U.S.A. in Your Chevrolet," words and music by Leon Carr and Leo Corday, Chappel & Co., by arrangement with H.R.H. Television Features Corporation and General Motors Corporation (Chevrolet Motors Division), red ground, pictures combination of twelve conductors, radio personalities, and singers associated with song, $15.

Sheet Music, Cole, "Cole 30 Flyer," words and music by J. Lee Bowers, published by the Henderson Motor Sales Company, Indianapolis, Indiana, advertisement on back for Model 30 Cole, 1910, $55–60.

Sheet Music, Ford, "The Ford: A March and Two-Step," Harry H. Zickel, published by the Ford Motor Car Company, advertisement on back picturing four models of Fords, copyright 1908, $50–60.

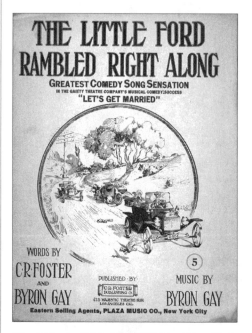

Sheet Music, Ford, "The Little Ford Rambled Right Along," by Byron Gay, Foster Publishing Company, marked on cover "Greatest comedy song sensation," 1914, $30. Although the lyrics tout the dependability of the Ford, it describes the car as a little "Road Louse."

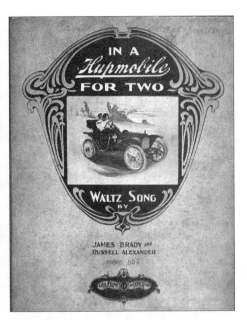

Sheet Music, Hupmobile, "In a Hupmobile for Two," by James Brady and Russell Alexander, Leo Feist Publisher, 1910, $50.

Sheet Music, "The Packard and the Ford: A Love Story," comic song, lyrics by Harry Carroll, Shapiro/Bernstein Music Publishing Company, 1915, $45–50.

Sheet Music, Mercer, "In My Mercer Racing Car," words and music by John S. Meck and Axel Christensen, published by Axel Christensen, compliments of the Simplex and Mercer Pacific Coast Agency, 1913, $60–70.

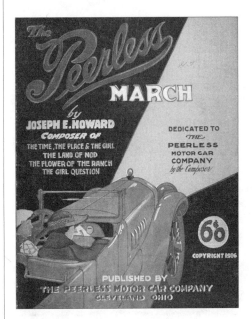

Sheet Music, Peerless, "The Peerless March," Joseph E. Howard, dedicated to the Peerless Motor Car Company by the composer, published by the Peerless Motor Car Company, Cleveland, Ohio, 1916, $45–50.

Sheet Music, generic, "The Lady Chauffeur," Intermezzo by Arthur Hauk, published by Joseph Morris Company, Philadelphia, Pennsylvania, 1917, $35.

Poster stamps are miniature versions of full-sized posters. These stamps were used on envelopes, invoices, and invitations that promoted automobile shows. Europeans loved them, especially in the late 19th and early 20th centuries. By 1910, Americans had fallen in love with them as well.

Stamp, poster, Buick, $15–20.

Stamp, poster, Chandler, $15–20.

Stamps, poster, Cleveland Auto Show, *(upper left)* December 30–January 7; *(upper right)* January 22–29; *(lower left)* January 21–28; *(lower right)* January 16–23; $15–20 each.

Stamp, poster, Cleveland Auto Show, January 19–27, $15–20.

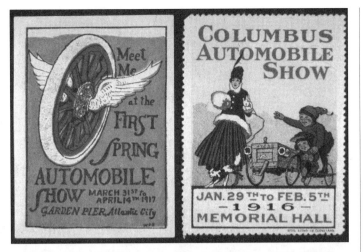

Stamps, poster, *(left)* First Spring Automobile Show, Atlantic City, 1917, $15–20; *(right)* Columbus Automobile Show, 1916, $15–20.

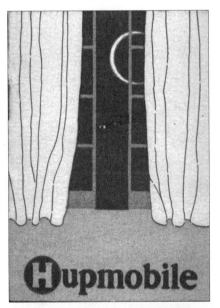

Stamps, poster, Hupmobile issued a set of twelve stamps housed in a stiff paper cover, each stamp valued at $15–20, cover valued at $25.

Stamp, poster, Overland, 1915, $15–20.

Stamp, poster, Packard, $15–20.

Stamps, poster, racing: *(upper left)* Indianapolis; *(upper right)* Astor Cup, 1915; *(lower left)* Nacional De Locutores; *(lower center)* Course de Cote; *(lower right)* Lugio, 1929; $15–20 each.

Stamps, poster, tire and accessory manufacturers: *(upper left)* Miller; *(upper right)* Fisk; *(upper center)* Goodrich; *(bottom left)* Firestone; *(bottom right)* Puritan Tires; $15–20 each.

Stamps, poster, accessory manufacturers: *(upper left)* Boyce Motor Meters; *(upper center)* Alloy Springs; *(upper right)* Mazda Lamps; *(lower left)* Walden Wrenches; *(lower right)* Hyatt Bearings; $15–20 each.

Stereoview Card, Model "T", 1913, $10–15.

Stock Certificate, Ben Hur Motor Company (1916–18, Willoughby, OH), $40–45.

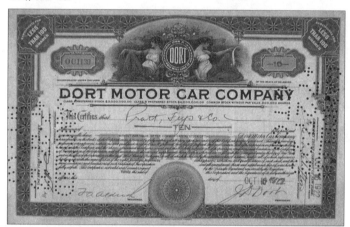

Stock Certificate, Dort (1015–24, Flint, Michigan), 1922, $35–40.

Stock Certificate, Jackson (1903–23, Jackson, Michigan), $40–45.

Stock Certificate, Peerless (1900–31, Cleveland, Ohio), 1927, $40–45.

Stock Certificate (1908–63, Toledo, Ohio), Willys-Overland, $35–40.

Stock Certificate, Pierce Arrow (1901–38, Buffalo, NY), $35–40.

Stock Certificate, Budd Wheel Company (Philadelphia, Pennsylvania), $25–30.

Tobacco Cards

Stock Certificate, U.S. Automobile Company, pictures Lexington automobile on certificate (1909–10, Lexington, Kentucky; 1911–28, Connersville, Indiana), 1920, $40–45.

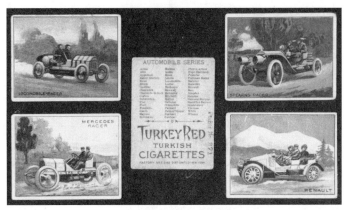

Tobacco Cards, Turkey Red Cigarettes, 50-card automobile series, selection of cards, 2" x 2 5/8", $1.50–2 each.

Tobacco Cards, B.G.H.L. Auto Cards, selection of cards from larger series, $1.50–2 each.

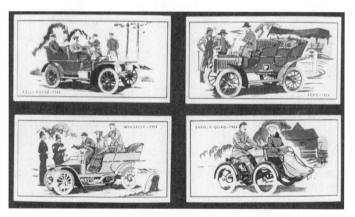

Tobacco Card Type, cards marked on back "Royal Society for the Prevention of Accidents," 24-card series, selection of cards, 1 3/8" x 2 1/4", $1.50–2 each.

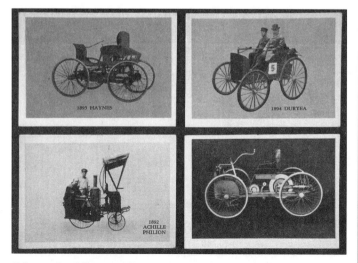

Tobacco Card Type, trading cards, manufactured by Oak Manufacturing Company, Culver City, California, selection of cards from larger series, 3 3/4" x 2 5/8", $1.50–2 each.

Two types of valentines are featured here—penny dreadfuls and postcards. Penny dreadfuls were nasty valentine broadsides, printed in a small poster format; 7 1/2" x 9" is about average. There were larger and smaller examples. Most valentine postcards date between 1900 and 1915, the Golden Age of the postcard.

Do not overlook children's school valentine cards, both folding and die cut, from the 1920s through the 1960s. Many of these have an automobile theme. Cost rarely exceeds a dollar or two. Expect to pay a premium for cards with mechanical action.

Valentine, penny dreadful, A Donkey's Role Is to Draw a Cart. Not to Run an Automobile, 7" x 9 1/2", circa 1900, $15–20.

A Donkey's role is to draw a cart. Not to run an automobile!
This is just a little picture of what is bound to come to pass,
when an Auto has for driver an unmitigated Ass.
That it has not happened yet to you, is sheer good luck, no doubt;
It's safe to bet it won't be long before it comes about.

Valentine, penny dreadful, The Auto Fiend, 7" x 9 5/8", 1920s, $10–15.

An automaniac, that's what you are!
You mortgaged your home to buy a bum car.
You rattle along at a dangerous speed,
And never the helpless pedestrians heed.
Your car's full of cranks and of nuts and what not,
But you are the crankiest nut of the lot.
They'll arrest you for speeding and put you in jail
That's where they cure Auto Fiends without fail.

Valentine, penny dreadful, Fliver Fiend, marked "Made in U.S.A.," 7 1/4" x 10 1/8", circa 1915, $5–10.

Although it's with apparent pride
That in your "lizzie" 'round you ride,
It's just an eyesore on the street,
Which passing motorists always greet
With a derisive grin and stare.
The junk pile's waiting. Dump it there.

Valentine, penny dreadful type, Tuck Company, England, Wheels, 1900s, $25.

Valentine, postcard, The Autoist, 1900s, $5.

When you go out with your new car
You don't quite know just where you are,
Whatever goes wrong, whether crank or spark,
As to how to fix it you're in the dark.

Valentine, postcard, The Automobile Fiend, 1907, $5.

Valentine, postcard, Garage: Repairing Automobiles A Cinch/Rank Extortion, 1920s, $4.

We charge our customers for three times what the job is worth. We have instructed our mechanics to add three hours to every one worked on our patrons' autos 'cause we need the dough. So now What Are You Going to Do About It?

Our Mechanics are all good liars at our request. If they they [sic] do one hour's work on your car we charge you for three hours.

Graft / Easy Money

Auto Owners. What Can We Do?

We put up a kick on our bills, but will have to put up

There seems no way to stop this gouge.

Valentine, postcard, Chauffeur, 1900s, $5.

*As a chauffeur
You're a loafer,
And you cannot run a car.
You're a grafter,
Fore and after.
As a failure, you're a star.*

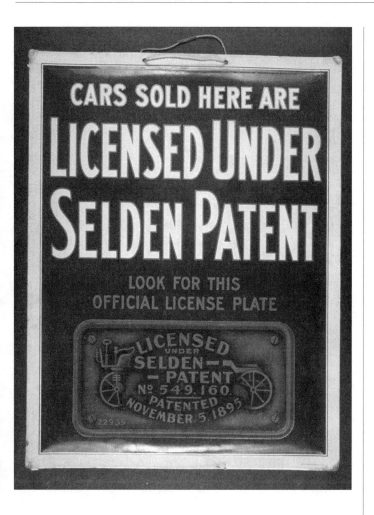

Window Display, Selden Patent, sign that member dealer could display in showroom, $275–300. In 1895 George B. Selden, Rochester, New York, was granted a patent covering all vehicles propelled by an internal combustion engine. He claimed he developed a gasoline-engine propelled car in 1877. In 1899 the Electrical Vehicle Company acquired the patent from Selden and formed the Associates of Licensed Automobile Manufacturers (A.L.A.M.) in 1903. This group sued Henry Ford. Ford fought the suit in the courts for eight years. In 1911 a ruling was issued declaring the Selden patent was valid for two-cycle engines but not four-cycle engines, the type used by Ford and almost all other manufacturers by 1910.

9.

PLAYTHINGS

Toys are the adult world in miniature. A great many past historical events have inspired manufacturers to make toys that commemorate them. Miniature guillotines, for example, were made during the French Revolution and given to children of soldiers who fought in the Revolution. A German company made a lithograph tin car featuring Buffalo Bill (William) Cody as the driver during his Wild West Show's tour of France.

A very short time separated the invention of the automobile and the first appearance of an automobile toy. By the early 1900s the automobile had gained significantly in popularity and so had the automobile toy, both cars and trucks.

Germany and France were the centers for early automobile development. As a result, the earliest automobile toys also originated in those countries. After World War I, the production of automobile toys shifted to the United States. By the mid-1920s cast-iron toys dominated. Arcade, Dent, Hubley, and Kenton are a few of the magic names. By the mid-1930s, pressed steel and lithograph tin toys challenged the cast-iron toy for dominance. Buddy L, Keystone, and Kingsbury are among the leading pressed steel toy manufacturers.

Because of my personal interest in pre–World War II automobiles, many of the images date from that period. Having noted this, I am aware that much of the action in the automobile toy market in the mid-1990s revolves around the buying and selling of post-1945 die-cast vehicles. The market has reached a level of sophistication where there is a separate price guide for every maker. Check with your local bookstore or antiques and collectibles bookseller to locate books of interest to you.

This chapter also includes games and jigsaw puzzles, two categories including items that remain very affordable. The keys are the surface image and condition. Some pre–World War II material is becoming pricey, especially if it has strong crossover collector interest. Post-1945 items are where the bargains can be found.

Cars and Other Toy Vehicles

CAST IRON

Cast iron, Arcade Mfg. Company, Freeport, Illinois, center door Model "T" Ford sedan, black painted body, silver-colored wheels, nickel-plated driver, 6 1/2" long, 4 1/4" high, circa 1920s, $850–900. Arcade was incorporated in 1885. In 1920 the company's slogan was "They Look Real." Arcade designed and made toy vehicles to resemble as closely as possible the actual car itself.

Cast iron, Arcade, center door Model "T" Ford sedan, green painted body, black undercarriage, silver-colored wheels, nickel-plated driver, 6 1/2" long, 4 1/4" high, circa 1920s, $850–900.

Cast iron, Arcade, pickup truck, red body, nickel-plated wheels, 8 1/2" long, late 1920s, $450–500.

Cast iron, Arcade, gasoline truck, marked "Mack," AC Mack cab, iron wheels, 14" long, iron wheels with rubber tires, circa late 1920s, $1,750–2,000.

Cast iron, Champion Hardware Company, Geneva, Ohio, AC Mack wrecker, red body, rubber wheels, 9" from hood to end of boom, circa 1930s, $450–500.

Cast iron, Champion, Stake body truck, blue body, nickel-plated wheels, 7 1/2" long, 3 1/2" high, $275–300.

Cast iron, Dent Hardware Co., Fullerton, Pennsylvania, Amos 'n' Andy, 5" long, $900–1,000. These toys were found unassembled at the Dent factory after it closed its doors. Nine were found, assembled, and painted with paint found in the Dent factory.

Cast iron, Dent, public service bus, Mack truck–like body with roof vents, brown body with black roof, nickel-plated wheels, gold trim, 14" long, $1,750–2,000. The Mack Company was located approximately ten miles from the Dent Hardware Company.

Cast iron, Dent, Bus Line, school bus, bright orange body, roof light, 8 1/2" long, 1920s, $450–500.

Cast iron, Jones and Bixler, Kenton, Ohio, Red Devil, open touring car, yellow color, 9" long, before 1910, $1,100–1,200. Jones and Bixler became Kenton in 1910. Bixler served as a toy designer in the late 1890s for Shimer Hardware Manufacturing Co., Freemansburg, Pennsylvania.

Cast iron, Hubley Manufacturing Company, Lancaster, Pennsylvania, Auto Express, open body truck, red body, yellow wheels, black driver, 9 1/2" long, circa 1910, $850–900. Hubley ceased toy manufacturing in 1978.

Cast iron, Kenton Hardware Manufacturing Company, Kenton, Ohio, horseless carriage, clockwork, black body with red trim, circa 1900, $1,250–1,500. Resembles an early steam horseless carriage. Wind-up cast-iron automobiles were intended to compete with the German and French tin automobiles.

Cast iron, Kenton, Jaeger Mixer, cast-iron truck, body painted red, nickel-plated drum mixer, rubber tires, 9 1/4" long, early 1930s, $550–600. Sold in 1932 for $1.

Cast iron, Kilgore, Westerville, Ohio, and some subsidiary manufacturing in Lancaster, Pennsylvania, and Canada, Arctic ice-cream truck. Blue chassis, red truck body, nickel-plated wheels, circa late 1920s, $600–650. Years ago I met the son of the owner of Kilgore Toys. While home from college in 1928, his father told him to do something for the company, and he designed the toy ice-cream truck.

Cloth, Racemates, EPI Marketing, 1996, teddy bear (Richard Petty's STP No. 43), 9" high, reverses itself and turns into NASCAR racing car (Rusty Wallace's Ford Motorsports' No. 2), 13" long and 7" high, $15–20.

CLOCKWORK

Clockwork, tin, A.O., French, "Automobile–Accident," 7 7/8" long, circa 1910, $2,750–3,000. As the car moves forward, it blows apart, throwing the driver and mechanic in the air.

Clockwork, pressed steel, ACME, Chicago, Illinois, Curved Dash Oldsmobile, 11" long, circa 1903, $950–1,000. The real Curved Dash Oldsmobile was a well-designed, simple automobile whose slogan was "All you have to do is watch the road." A critic said, "Yes, but from under the car."

Clockwork, tin, Arnold, marked "Western Germany," Tin Lizzy, remote control, 9 3/4" long, circa 1950s, $225–250.

Clockwork, tin, Japanese, marked with a "B" trademark, MG-like car, red body, 1954, $125–150.

Clockwork, lithograph tin, Bing German, limousine, black body with red pinstriping, 13" long, $2,250–2,500.

Clockwork, lithograph tin, Bing, limousine, red body, black fenders, gold trim, 12" long, circa 1915, $2,500–3,000.

Clockwork, lithograph tin, Hans Eberl, German, "Confrontation Car," 11 1/8" long, circa 1910, $2,500–3,000. When put in motion, the cow strikes the car radiator, not an unusual event during the early days of motoring. There is a jester logo on both rear doors.

Clockwork, Carette, German, #50 touring car, 9 5/8"
long, $2,500–3,000.

Clockwork, lithograph tin, Carette, limousine, passenger in the rear
compartment wearing fur stole, 10 1/4" long, circa 1910,

Clockwork, lithograph tin, Carette, limousine, dark green body with
red pinstriping, front wheels adjust so automobile can run in circle,
12 3/8" long, circa 1915, $3,500–4,000.

Clockwork, lithograph tin, Carette, limousine, green body with gold
trim, rubber tires, 7 1/2" long, $1,750–2,000. This is the smallest size
of this style limousine.

Clockwork, painted sheet steel, Corcoran Manufacturing Company
(1920 through 1940s), Washington, Indiana, Cor Cor, 1935 Graham
Paige, deep maroon body, nickel-plated hubcaps and bright work,
rubber tires, 20" long, $1,000–1,250.

Clockwork, lithographed tin, Gilbert, American, Racer, yellow body
with black trim, crank winds spring, 9 1/2" long, circa 1915,
$325–350. Appeared in Sears, Roebuck catalog for $0.59.

Clockwork, lithographed tin, Guntherman (ASGW), German, Gordon Bennett race car, painted figures, 11 3/4" long, $10,000–15,000. Copied racer with shamrock on its hood that participated in a race in Ireland sponsored by Gordon Bennett, an American publisher.

Clockwork, lithograph tin, friction, Hess, touring car, composition figure, circa 1910, $750–800. Turn crank and push down on steering wheel to set car in motion.

Clockwork, lithograph tin, Guntherman, Vis-a-Vis style body, black body, hand-painted figure, rubber tires, 11 3/8" long, circa 1900, $2,750–3,000.

Clockwork, painted tin, Jouet de Paris, French, deluxe limousine, red body, 15" long, circa 1908, $3,000–3,500.

Clockwork, lithograph tin, friction, Hess, Nuremberg, German, Hessmobil, 8 7/8" long, $950–1,000.

Clockwork, painted tin, Jouet de Paris, French, race car, white body, rubber tires, circa 1904, $1,750–2,000.

Clockwork, Kingsbury, American, Blue Bird Racer, blue body, $1,500–1,750. The Blue Bird raced at Daytona Beach, Florida. The actual racer is in the National Motor Museum in Beaulieu, England, the site of Europe's largest auto jumble (flea market/car show).

Clockwork, lithograph tin, Ernst Lehman, German, (left) Also and (right) LoLo, circa 1910, $275–300 each. Ernst Lehman belonged to a society of humorists whose members used comical phrases as toasts. Lehman used some of these toasts as names for his tin toys.

Clockwork, lithograph tin, Lehman, Motor Kutsche, 4 7/8" long, circa 1910, $450–500.

Clockwork, lithographic tin, Lehman, Tut-Tut, white body, red trim, man blows horn as car moves forward erratically, 16 3/4" long, $900–1,000. One of the most popular lithograph tin toys in the Lehman line. Made for several decades.

Clockwork, painted tin, Martin, French, Victorian motorized carriage, black body, 14 1/2" long, circa 1900, $2,750–3,000.

Clockwork, lithograph tin, Marx, Erie, Pennsylvania, Amos 'n' Andy Fresh Air Taxi, car moves forward and goes into stall that shakes Amos, the driver, and dog in the front seat and Andy, who is smoking his cigar and seated in the back, 8" long, circa 1930, $900–1,000.

Clockwork, Moses Kohnstam, German, Moko, 4-cylinder motor with moving pistons, forward and reverse action, circa late 1920s, $700–750. Sold for $0.95 in 1927 Montgomery Ward catalog.

Clockwork, lithograph tin, Japanese, marked "Japan/S.S.S.," sedan with blue body, trailer with silver body, trailer contains picnic table and chairs, circa 1950s, $150–175.

Clockwork, lithograph tin, Tellus Company, German, Auto Polo, 6 3/4" long, circa 1913, $900–1,000. Most cars used in motor polo were converted Model "T" Fords. Local fairgrounds were the most popular sites for auto polo games.

Clockwork, lithograph tin, Japanese, marked with "Y" trademark, Corvair sedan, blue body, windshield wiper moves as the car moves forward, circa 1950s, $125–150.

Clockwork, painted tin, unknown maker (possibly Carette), Amphibian, boat-like vehicle with wheels, each rear wheel of two-disk construction with baffles between the disks that serve as paddles, circa 1910, $1,250–1,500.

Clockwork, lithograph tin, German, hansom cab, circa 1900, $650–750.

Clockwork, lithograph tin, Japanese, no trademark, touring car, light blue body, rubber tires, circa 1950s, $150–175.

Die Cast

Samuel Dowst, a trade journal publisher, adapted a lead type-casting machine to make small promotional miniatures. By 1911 he had produced a small 77mm limousine. A 77mm Ford Model "T" followed in 1914. By the late 1920s was a full line of toy vehicles being manufactured. The Tootsie Toy trade name came from Dowst's daughter, Tootsie.

Die Cast, Matchbox, 1:75 scale, *(top left)* 5C-2, London Bus, introduced 1961, red body, 2 9/16" long, $35; *(top right)* 58C-1, DAF Girder Truck, introduced in 1968, white body, orange girders, 3" long, $10; *(bottom left)* 39C-1 Ford Tractor, introduced in 1967, 2 1/8" long, $12; *(bottom right)* 41C-3, Ford GT, introduced in 1965, white body, 2 5/8" long, $14.

Die cast, Tootsie Toy, "Funnies" series, Moon Mullins in a police wagon, blue body, yellow wheels, mechanical action, circa 1932, $225–250.

Die cast, Tootsie Toy, Graham roadster, orange body, brown fenders, six wheels, circa 1934, $90–100.

Many other companies, including Corgi and Dinky, made die-cast toys. These companies are covered in detail in general and specific toy price guides.

ELECTRIC

Electric, battery powered, lithograph tin, Japanese, marked "Japan/ Sign of Quality/'B'," Oldsmobile Toranado, gold body, retracting light covers, $150–175.

Electric, painted tin, battery operated, Carlisle and Finch Company, 10" long, 7 1/2" high, $4,500–5,000. Pictured in the 1901 Carlisle and Finch catalog with the slogan: "Electricity will undoubtedly be the universal method of propulsion for all vehicles in the near future." Sold initially for $3.50.

Electric, battery operated, lithograph tin, Knapp Electric Company, New York, New York, Electric Automobile, rear wheels powered by small electric motor using a dry cell battery as a power source, adjust steering wheel to make car go forward or in a circle, rubber tires, 12" long, 6" deep, 7 1/2" high to top of back of seat where driver would sit, circa 1900, $2,250–2,500. Also distributed via the Carlisle and Finch catalog.

Electric, Lionel Company, New York, New York, Lionel race set, one racer with red body, other racer with orange body, each with composition figure of driver and mechanic, cars race on a grooved track, center rail provides the power source, 8" long, 1911 to 1913, $1,250–1,500.

Electric, painted sheet steel, Ko Ko Mo - Stamped Metal Company, American, similar in appearance to 1925 Chrysler, yellow body, powered via a rail attached to a fence that flanks track, 10 3/4" long, late 1920s, $325–350.

Electric, Ko Ko Mo - Stamped Metal Company, futuristic racer, red body, powered via a rail attached to a fence that flanks track, 14 1/2" long, circa 1930s, $325–350.

PENNY TOYS

Penny Toys, most of which were manufactured in Germany, came in a wide variety of shapes—animals, automobiles, boats, mechanical equipment, people, planes, etc. Few contain manufacturer's markings.

Penny Toy, lithograph tin, German, limousine, blue body with yellow trim, chauffer and passengers, 4 1/2" wide, 2 3/8" high, circa 1905, $125–150.

Penny Toy, lithograph tin, German, open touring car, white body with gold trim, 4 1/2" wide, 2" high, circa 1910, $125–150.

PLASTIC

Plastic, Cadbury's, advertising, Creme Egg Motor Van, red and blue plastic body, 2 3/4" long, mid-1990s, $2.

Plastic, Kenner, Smash-Up Derby, 1973, two special fly-apart SSP (Super Sonic Power) cars, two jump ramp/barriers, two "T" handle power sticks, box measures 17 1/2" x 11 3/4" x 3", $50.

Plastic, Hess, 1975, marked "Made in Hong Kong" and "Amerada Hess Corporation" on bottom, battery-operated head- and taillights (instruction card explains where and how to install battery), 14" long, truck, barrels, and instruction sheet—$150; mint in box—$250.

Plastic, Hess, 1991, toy truck and racer, battery operated head- and taillights, racer with friction motor, $25–30.

SILVER

Clockwork, French, sterling silver, taxi, 7" wide, 5" high, circa 1910, $3,000–3,500.

STEAM

Steam, painted sheet steel, Doll, German, maroon body with red pinstriping, boiler and engine under the hood that produce live steam, four cast wheels, rubber tires, rear-drive automobile, 19" long, circa 1925, $4,500–5,000.

Steam, lithograph tin, Ernst Plank, German, all black, composition driver, 8" long, circa 1895, $1,750–2,000.

Steam, wood, Schoenhut, Philadelphia, Pennsylvania, Auto Build Kit, five toys in one, build either coupe, delivery wagon, limousine, racer, or roadster, finished roadster measures 11 1/4" wide and 4 1/2" high, circa 1925, $125–150.

Games

It is often the boxed board game lid graphics that make a game collectible, as opposed to the playing board and pieces inside. Pre-1915 game box lids feature some of the finest lithography of the period.

Automobile-related games were produced primarily in England, France, Germany, and the United States. A number of early French games had great board game covers, like "La Coupe Gordon Bennett," showing a circa 1905 race car, and "Le Tour de Monde Automobile," a road tour through Africa.

Classic American boxed board game covers include McLoughlin Brothers' "The Horseless Carriage Race" (1900), "The Automobile Race" (1904), "The Vanderbilt Cup of 1907," and Milton Bradley's "Automobile Race Game."

Game, boxed board, track, Selchow and Righter, Huggin' the Rail, realistic auto race game, lid pictures a late 1940s race car, $50–60.

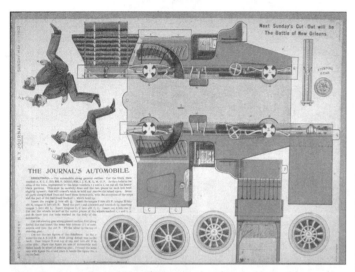

Cutout, art supplement feature, *New York Journal and American,* May 11, 1902, $50–75.

Game, boxed board, track, Milton Bradley, No. 4254, Smitty, box lid cartoon illustration by Bernd shows Smitty in the backseat of car blowing a horn, driver thinks someone is trying to pass him, box measures 16 1/2" x 8 1/2" x 3/4", mid-1930s, $65–75.

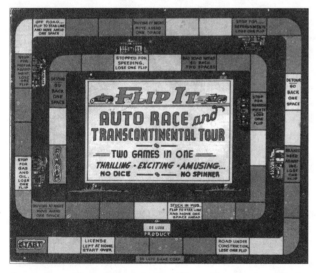

Game, boxed board, track, Deluxe Game Corporation, Flip It Auto Race, combines auto race and transcontinental tour, $65–75.

Game, boxed board, track, Milton Bradley, No 4516, Walt & Skeezix Gasoline Alley Game, box measures 19 1/4" x 10" x 1 5/8", circa mid-1920s, $100–125. Gasoline Alley was Frank King's comic strip, syndicated by the *Chicago Tribune.* Skeezix was Walt's nephew.

Puzzles

There are several varieties of automobile-related puzzles: (1) advertising premium puzzles issued by automobile manufacturers and distributors, (2) advertising premium puzzles issued by gasoline and other automobile support companies, (3) generic puzzles with an automobile image or an automobile as part of the overall image, (4) puzzles in children's sets that have an automobile theme, and (5) souvenir puzzles. Of these types, the advertising premium puzzles are the most desirable, followed by early wood generic puzzles with an automobile surface image.

Advertising, die cut, composition board, Chevrolet, Picture Puzzles—Fun for Children/For Economical Transportation, box and set of two puzzles; each puzzle has twelve pieces and measures 6 1/2" x 4 1/2", box measures 6 7/8" x 4 5/8" x 7/8", mid-1920s, $300–350 for complete unit (box and two puzzles).

Box lid, Superior Chevrolet 5-Passenger Sedan.

Advertising, pseudo wood, Baker Electric, car in snow scene, thirty-five pieces, 7 1/4" x 5", one-of-a-kind (amateur cutter used advertisement as puzzle subject), circa 1918, $150–200.

Puzzle, Superior Chevrolet Utility Coupe.

Puzzle, Superior Chevrolet 5-Passenger Touring.

Advertising, die cut, cardboard, Chevrolet, 1967 Camaro, folder format, frame tray puzzle within, red body, 25 pieces, folded measures 6 3/4" x 4 7/8", dealer's imprint on back, $15–20.

Advertising, wood, A. W. Harris Oil Company, Providence, Rhode Island, Harris Oil, roadside billboard "Make for easy running," circa 1905, $90–100.

Advertising, die cut, cardboard, Crisco Racing, Burt Bodine and the Crisco Thunderbird stock car, full-color image, 200 pieces, 17" x 11", $20–25. Received as a premium in the store for buying one three-pound Crisco Shortening or one forty-eight-ounce Crisco Oil.

Puzzle, wood, Mosaic Art Picture Puzzles, The Shop at the Inn, illustration by Walter Apperson Clark, copyright 1905 by P. F. Collier and Sons, $90–100. Walter A. Clark was one of the best early automobile artists. He was killed in an automobile accident.

BIBLIOGRAPHY

Anderton, Mark, and Sherry Mullen. *Gas Station Collectibles.* Radnor, PA: Wallace-Homestead Book Co., 1994.

Benjamin, Scott, and Wayne Henderson. *Gas Pump Globes: Collector's Guide to Over 3,000 American Gas Globes.* Osceola, WI: Motorbooks International, 1993.

———. *Oil Company Signs: A Collector's Guide.* Osceola, WI: Motorbooks International, 1995.

Butler, Steve, and Clarence Young. *Autoquotes—The Complete Reference for Promotional Pot Metal & Plastic with Prices.* York, PA, and Weaverville, NC: Autohobby Books, 1993.

Clymer, Floyd. *Those Wonderful Old Automobiles.* New York, Bonanza Books, 1953.

———. *Treasury of Early American Automobiles, 1877–1925.* New York: McGraw Hill Book Company, 1950.

Crisler, Bob. *License Plate Values: A Guide to Relative Prices of Collectible U.S. Auto License Plates and Their Grading.* Arrington, TN: King Publishing Co., 1994.

Gottschalk, Lillian. *American Toy Cars & Trucks.* New York: Abbeville Press, 1985.

Gunnell, John A. *A Collector's Guide to Automobilia.* Iola, WI: Krause Publications, 1994.

O'Brien, Richard. *Collecting Toys: A Collector's Identification & Value Guide, No. 7.* Florence, AL: Books Americana, 1995.

Pease, Rick. *Filling Station Collectibles with Price Guide.* Atglen, PA: Schiffer Publishing, 1994.

———. *Service Station Collectibles.* Atglen, PA: Schiffer Publishing, 1996.

Poulain, Hervé. *L'art et l'automobile.* Zourg (Swiss): Les clefs dup temps, 1973.

Pressland, David. *The Art of the Tin Toy.* London: New Cavendish, 1976.

Prior, Rupert (comp.). *Motoring: The Golden Years: A Pictorial Anthology: The Khachadourian Gallery.* London: H. C. Blossoms, Ltd., 1991.

Remise, Jac, and Jean Fondin. *The Golden Age of Toys.* Switzerland, 1967. A selection of the International Book Society, a division of Time-Life Books; distributed by New York Graphic Society Ltd., Greenwich, CT. English translation by D. B. Tubbs.

Schaut, Jim and Nancy. *American Automobilia: An Illustrated History and Price Guide.* Radnor, PA: Wallace-Homestead Book Company, 1994.

Smith, Dan. *Accessory Mascots: The Automotive Accents of Yesteryear, 1910–1940.* San Diego, CA: Published by author, 1989.

Summers, B. J., and Wayne Priddy. *Value Guide to Gas Station Memorabilia.* Paducah, KY: Collector Books, 1995.

Tubbs, D. B. *Art and the Automobile.* London: Arlington Press, a Quarto Book, 1978.

Worthington-Williams, Michael. *Automobilia: A Guide Tour for Collectors.* London: BT Botsford and the Royal Automobile Club, 1979. American edition published by Hastings House Publishers, New York, in 1979.

Zolomij, John. *The Motorcar in Art.* Kutztown, PA: Automobile Quarterly Publications, 1990.

PERIODICALS

Automobile Quarterly, PO Box 348, Kutztown, PA 19530

Hemming's Motor News, PO Box 100, Bennington, VT 05201

Mobilia, PO Box 575, Middlebury, VT 05753

Old Cars, 700 East State Street, Iola, WI 54990

COLLECTORS' CLUBS

Antique Automobile Club of America, Inc., PO Box 417, Hershey, PA 17033

Classic Car Club of America, 1645 Des Plaines River Road, Ste. 7, Des Plaines, IL 60018

The Horseless Carriage Club of America, 128 S. Cypress Street, Orange, CA 92666

Society of Automotive Historians, PO Box 339, Matamora, PA 18336

Veteran Motor Car Club of America, PO Box 360788, Strongsville, OH 44136

MUSEUMS

Auburn-Cord-Duesenberg Museum, 1600 South Wayne Street, Auburn, IN 46706

Behring Automotive Museum, 3700 Blackhawk Plaza Circle, Danville, CA 14506

Frederick C. Crawford Auto-Aviation Museum, 10825 East Blvd., Cleveland, OH 44106

Henry Ford Museum, 20900 Oakwood Blvd., Dearborn, MI 48120

Harrah's Automobile Collection, Glendale Road, Reno, NV 89504

Heritage Plantation Auto Museum, Grove and Pine Streets, Sandwich, MA 02563

Imperial Palace Auto Collection, 3535 Las Vegas Blvd., Las Vegas, NV 89109

Los Angeles Museum of Natural History, Exhibition Park, 900 Exhibition Blvd., Los Angeles, CA 90007

Museum of American History, Smithsonian Institution, Washington, DC 20560

Museum of Science and Industry, 57th and Lakeshore Drive, Chicago, IL 60637

Merle Norman Classic Beauty Collection, 15180 Bledsoe Street, San Sylmar, CA 91342

The Owls Head Transportation Museum, Knox County Airport, Owls Head, ME 04854

Pate Museum of Transportation, U.S. Highway 377, Fort Worth, TX 76101

Pettits Museum of Motoring Memories, Louisa, VA 23093

Pioneer Auto Museum, Murdo, SD 57559

Swigart Museum, Museum Park, Huntingdon, PA 16652

AUCTION HOUSES

Barrett-Jackson, 5530 East Washington, Phoenix, AZ 85034

Rich Cole Auctions, 10701 Riverside Drive, North Hollywood, CA 91602

Kruse International, PO Box 190, Auburn, IN 46706

Spectrum Vehicle Auctions, 18000 Devonshire Street, Northridge, CA 91325

ABOUT THE AUTHOR

DAVID K. BAUSCH is a leading collector of antique automobiles, automobilia, automobile toys, and related paper ephemera. Various parts of his collection have been featured in national and trade periodicals and newspapers. In addition, he has authored several dozen articles related to the topics upon which he collects. He appears regularly on television and radio programs relating to collecting.

Mr. Bausch has served four terms as County Executive for Lehigh County, Pennsylvania. Prior to that he had a distinguished career as a hospital administrator. He is also a retired sergeant major of the U.S. Air Force Medical Corps.

COLLECTOR CARS ARE HOT!

Ride down memory lane with *The Official Price Guide to Collector Cars*. This comprehensive guide includes

- current market values for every model and every manufacturer in the United States and abroad through the mid-1970s, including Ford, Buick, Chevy, Packard, Ferrari, and Mercedes-Benz

- important tips on buying, selling, and restoring collector cars

- fully illustrated, PLUS an insert featuring cars from the National Automobile Museum in Reno, Nevada

- special section includes trucks and motorcycles

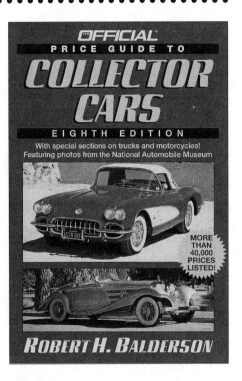

HOUSE OF COLLECTIBLES
SERVING COLLECTORS FOR MORE THAN THIRTY-FIVE YEARS